# GOLDEN
# RETRIEVERS

Kennel Stud Book, kept by
Dudley Coutts Marjoribanks (1820-1894)
(son of Edward Marjoribanks
of Stanmore Park Mx. & Greenlands, Bucks.
partner in Coutts' Bank 1796 — 1868)
ed. Harrow & Ch. Ch. Oxford
partner in Coutts' Bank & Meux Brewery
m. 1848 Isabella, d. of Sir James
Weir Hogg M.P.; was M.P.
for Berwick 1853 — 1881; created
a Baronet 1866 and Baron
Tweedmouth in 1881.
    This book is given to the
Kennel Club Library by his
grand-daughter Marjorie Lady Pentland
September 1963. Its special interest
lies in showing the origin of the
yellow, now called golden, retrievers,
which he bred at Guisachan, the
Invernessshire property he bought in 1854

# GOLDEN
# RETRIEVERS

Lyn Anderson

THE CROWOOD PRESS

First published in 2008 by
The Crowood Press Ltd
Ramsbury, Marlborough
Wiltshire SN8 2HR

www.crowood.com

Dedication
Per l'amore della mia vita

**British Library Cataloguing-in-Publication Data**
A catalogue record for this book is available from the British Library.

ISBN 978 1 84797 025 1

Frontispiece: Inscription from Lord Tweedmouth's stud book, now in the possession of the Kennel Club. Reproduced by permission of the Kennel Club Picture Library.

Typeset by Servis Filmsetting Ltd, Manchester

Printed and bound in India by Replika Press

# Contents

# 1 In the Beginning

Once a dog enters your home, life will never again be the same. No longer are you free to come and go as you please, because there is now an animal that is totally dependent on you for housing, feeding and general care. Holidays are no longer the carefree events they once were, because now either you will need to choose places where your dog can accompany you, or he will need to go into boarding kennels during your absence. There is also a third option, which is to have a dog sitter who will move into your home. My dogs are looked after in this way when I have a holiday, and I find it most satisfactory, as the upset to the dogs' routine is minimal.

Countless people are willing to have a permanent change in their lifestyle so they may enjoy the companionship of a dog. Usually what decides which breed is the chosen one, is how compatible the temperament of owners and dogs proves to be.

## Why Choose this Breed?

I once heard the Golden Retriever referred to as 'a dog for all reasons', and I have never found a description that improves on this. At his best, the Golden is a sweet-natured, gentle and trustworthy companion. He adores his family, and just about everyone

" We can use it as often as we like. We are the last she'd ever suspect "

*The media is partly responsible for the popularity of the breed.*

*The appeal of the breed is obvious.*

*Goldens will take all the exercise you can provide.*

The adult Golden will take all the exercise you can give him, and still be ready for more. Conversely, he is happy to sleep at your feet as you are reading, or lie beside you in the garden. Over forty years ago I was undecided whether to have a Saluki or a Golden Retriever, and very nearly decided against the latter as I read that the breed needed at least four miles of roadwork a day, as well as plenty of free running. Then I was lucky enough to hear an eminent breeder say that if half the owners of the breed took notice of the exercise requirements advocated in books, there would be many exhausted – even deceased! – owners! That decided me, and so I acquired my first Golden – and have been obsessed with the breed up until this very day.

else he meets. He is biddable and quick to learn, and generally doesn't mind what you teach him as long as his mind is occupied. He will participate in competitive obedience, agility and gundog work. His use as a guide dog is well known, and he will also act as an assistance dog to the disabled. He is an invaluable aid to his blind owner, and the Guide Dogs for the Blind Association have long used pure-bred Goldens, or Goldens crossed with Labradors, for this purpose.

It should never be forgotten that the Golden was bred to work, and he is never happier than when he is doing just that. To make him happy you don't have to put all your efforts into field trials, just let him do some carrying and searching. If the Golden has a fault, it is that he tends to do everything with great enthusiasm; this is especially

*The breed is never happier than when working.*

*Gardeners sometimes have a problem with their dogs' obsession with digging.*

*Attachments are formed between dogs and a variety of other animals.*

noticeable when visitors call, when if left unchecked he will greet them rapturously, and will jump up and lick their faces. The earlier he is trained to realize that this is not acceptable behaviour, the better.

Goldens tend to be quite vocal if strangers approach either their property or, say, the child they are with, but it never goes beyond being a warning. If you want a dog to guard your house, don't even consider this breed. If you are a keen gardener, sharing your lawn and flowerbeds with your dog will prove a challenge because Goldens are the most enthusiastic diggers, and it is not unusual to find several digging the same hole. The solution is to ensure the dog does not have access to the whole garden when unattended.

*Dogs and cats will live happily together if introduced when young.*

Goldens can learn to share their homes with other animals. I had a male who developed a life-long attachment to a ram, who was very sweet with the dog but quite murderous in his intentions towards me!

## The Origins of the Breed

Originally it was believed that the breed, as we know it, had been bred from a troupe of circus dogs. This makes a good story but is totally unsubstantiated. In fact the Guisachan estate in the Highlands is celebrated as the birthplace of the Golden Retriever. Today the house is a façade, with all behind in ruin, and over the last thirty years that I have visited this atmospheric and most beautiful site, the decay has been marked. There is just one moment, after entering through the gates, when the trees mask the ravages of time and it is possible to believe the house is still complete.

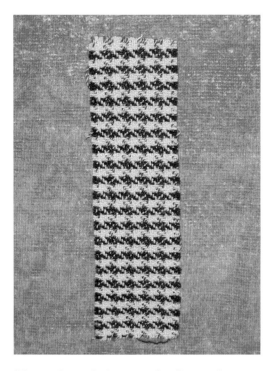

*The tweed worn by keepers and stalkers on the Guisachan estate.*

The whole estate was a model at the time it was built, and boasted many amenities not found elsewhere. The village of Tomich, built to house the estate workers, boasted new-fangled water closets that were not evident in other houses for many years to come.

This was the country residence of Sir Dudley Coutts Marjoribanks, a Member of Parliament, later to be known as Lord Tweedmouth. Although based in London, he hosted grand hunting parties, and the Tomich Hotel, which may be seen today, was his hunting lodge. Heads of state came as visitors, their stay at the house commemorated by trees planted in the grounds. It is reported that Sir Winston Churchill learned to drive on the estate.

Lord Tweedmouth and his son purchased a Yellow Retriever (the title 'Golden Retriever' was not yet recognized) in Brighton in the 1860s. This dog, called 'Nous', was the only yellow in an otherwise all black litter. The mating of this dog to a Tweed water spaniel called Belle in 1868, from which three

*The ruins of Guisachan house today.*

*Workers' cottages provided by Lord Tweedmouth.*

puppies resulted, formed the basis of the breed as we now know it.

Over the years until the last litter was produced at the end of the 1800s (Lord Tweedmouth died in 1894), various other breeds were introduced in the breeding programme, with the object of strengthening the working ability of the resulting dogs.

Lord Tweedmouth's son, the Hon. Archie Marjoribanks, moved to Canada taking a

*Tomich Hotel.*

11

bitch called Lady with him. On his death, his widow remarried and her son, Lord Hailsham (a future Lord Chancellor in Great Britain), remembered the 'new' breed of Golden Retrievers being discussed.

It is fortunate that Lord Tweedmouth's stud book survived: it is now kept in the Kennel Club, donated by Lady Pentland, Lord Tweedmouth's granddaughter. Tracing some of the pedigrees is diffcult in that many dogs' names were repeated in future litters – unlike today, when the name would have

*The bronze of Lord Tweedmouth on the fountain in Tomich.*

*Lady Tweedmouth's bronze on Tomich fountain.*

been preceded by an affix, so making clear exactly which dog or bitch is recorded.

I found records of Lord Tweedmouth's reputation as a respected breeder of Aberdeen Angus cattle in some old magazines recording show results. He was the archetypical landowner, but kinder to his workers than some. Ruins of the hydroelectric scheme he installed may still be seen today, as may the old dairy and kennelman's house (now, both are guest

*The ornate fountain in Tomich, erected in memory of Lord and Lady Tweedmouth.*

*The gates to Guisachan estate, showing the 'M' which was the insignia of the Marjoribanks family.*

*The kennels' house, where heated quarters were provided for the dogs.*

## The Ruin of Guisachan House

*The remains of the 100yd target.*

Many believed there had been a fire at the great house, causing the roof to collapse, but there never was a fire. Lady Islington ordered the removal of the roof when she found a naturist group frolicking there. It seemed a drastic action, as once the house was open to the elements, its decay would be certain and swift. Locals told me that houses for miles around sported mantelshelves and whole fireplaces made from stone from the ruins of Guisachan! It is shocking to learn that the main cause of the house's decay is that much of the interior was demolished with the sole purpose of selling the stone. The steps and balustrades, which feature in the earliest photographs of the dogs and keepers, went the same way.

Some of the furniture and fittings may be seen today in Guisachan Ranch in British Columbia. This was built by Lady Aberdeen, Lord Tweedmouth's daughter (whose husband was governor) as she found the countryside so reminiscent of that surrounding Giusachan House. Many of the wonderful trees and shrubs at Guisachan House were also taken to the ranch, where they may still be seen. A whole area is dedicated to preserving what previously existed in Scotland, at the Canadian Guisachan Heritage Park.

houses). It is interesting to note that Lord Tweedmouth was concerned that his dogs were relatively short-lived, and attributed this to the fact that when they returned wet from a hard day's work on the estate, they lay in cold, damp kennels. He relocated the kennels to the rear of the kennelman's house, where he installed heating in the form of hot air from charcoal burners. He found this solved the problem, and his dogs lived considerably longer.

The idea of centrally heated kennels is quite amazing, considering that such luxury in private houses would not be the norm for over sixty years. Guisachan boasted gas central heating that was produced on the estate; the indentations where the gasometers (made of metal and leather) stood are clearly visible today. The gas house now balances precariously on the edge of the river bank, whereas in Lord Tweedmouth's day it was situated well back.

## The Breed's More Recent Evolution

Initially the breed was truly dual purpose, which is to say it was worked and shown. Sadly, relatively few show dogs today are worked – though it may be argued that many of the original owners were better placed to work their dogs to the gun than the urban dwellers of today. Most belonged to the upper classes and were truly landed gentry. Lecturing on the breed abroad, I was amused when I was asked if having a double-barrelled name was a prerequisite of owning a Golden Retriever! Certainly this was true of a large percentage of owners in the beginning, but it had never occurred to me until then. Yellow Retrievers started to make their appearance in the show ring as well as in the field, but it was not until 1920 that they were entered as 'Golden Retrievers'.

When I first began to keep the breed, in 1965, it was quite common to find black

*Pale-coated Goldens are not as modern as is believed.*

spots and even larger black patches on puppies. I remember one proud owner telling me she had been charged more for her puppy because of his patch! There is little doubt that these densely pigmented areas are throwbacks to the time when other breeds were introduced to improve hunting and scenting ability. We know for certain that several of these breeds were dark-coated, so it is from here that such patches are inherited. I produced a litter by a champion dog over thirty years ago, where two of the puppies had large black spots, one on the cheek and the other under the chin. I was aghast, but the stud dog's owner told me it was a common occurrence. I have never seen such markings since, and I imagine the passage of time will so dilute the predisposition to this fault that it will totally disappear.

Those who dislike the very pale coat colour of the breed are adamant that this is a modern trend, but more experienced, much older breeders will recall some blond animals very early on. The colour debate has certainly been ongoing throughout my forty or so years' experience of the breed, and shows no sign of abating. One way to really annoy an owner is to describe his dog as being of a bad colour. However, it is said of a good horse that it can never be a bad colour, and the same is true of dogs: as long as the animal's coat is commensurate with the colour dictated by the breed standard as set out by the Kennel Club, then it cannot be incorrect.

## The Breed Standard

The standard is a blueprint for the breed but, like most written descriptions, has shortcomings. The 'broad' head and 'kind' expression required is open to personal interpretation. How broad is 'broad'? When does 'broad'

*Balance is an essential of the breed standard.*

become 'coarse'? A mastiff has a broad head, but such a head would be hugely out of proportion on a Golden.

Balance is the essence of the standard, with moderation in all things. It is not a breed of extremes, such as the Bulldog or Pekingese: it is a dog-shaped dog, constructed mindful of the purpose for which it was bred, namely as a gundog. A gundog would fail badly if it were too weak-jawed or short-necked to carry game; an adult cock pheasant is a heavy bird, and the dog must be able to jump a five-barred gate while carrying one. A hare is even heavier and is a long animal.

The reachy, muscular neck, coupled with the strong jaw of the Golden, enables him to hold his prey clear as he jumps. It is a salutary exercise to hold either a pheasant or hare aloft, in one hand, in order to feel the weight.

The eyes of the Golden Retriever should be dark brown. The required kind expression could never result if they are black or amber, as these extremes of eye colour give a hard expression, far from kindly in appearance. The same is true of eyes set too close together, or slanting.

Examine twenty Golden Retrievers and you will most probably find twenty different ear types. The desired size is 'moderate', but many tend to be rather large. What is not mentioned in the standard, but something that affects the balance of the head, is the thickness of the earflap, or pinna. This flap ranges from feeling like the thinnest chamois leather to resembling a thick triangle of felt. Ears that are too thin and pendulous are too much like a hound's in appearance, and the thick ones are equally uncharacteristic. A set which is too high or low is undesirable.

The prominence on top of the head is known as the occiput, and can be very prominent in puppies; if they knock the occiput, a swelling may result that can take several months to subside. The ideal proportions for the head are that it is of equal length from occiput to stop (the indentation between the eyes), as from the stop to the tip of the nose.

The way in which a dog's teeth fit together is called the 'bite'. Goldens are required to have a 'scissor bite', where the top teeth very slightly overlap the bottom. Only the edges of the teeth are involved, and the remainder of the bottom teeth should be clearly visible.

Nose colour is frequently a subject of discussion between owners. The standard requires that the nose be black, but a huge percentage of Goldens have brown, mottled (referred to as a 'Dudley' nose) or pink noses. Some regain darker pigment in summer, but others never do. The colour of a puppy's nose is no guide to the adult colour. Moreover it is an amazing fact that bitches with the palest of pigment will have the blackest nose imaginable within a few days of whelping, but by the time the pups are eight weeks old, it will have reverted to its former colour.

There have been many champion dogs and bitches with other than black noses. Some think it is a serious fault, but I believe it to be a relatively minor one, as it does not affect the

*Noses should be black.*

*The forelegs should be straight.*

*The author's well constructed bitch, aged two years.*

*A show champion male, owned and bred by the author, illustrating the desired level topline and tail-set.*

dog's health, nor mar his working ability. I would also say that there is little that is more attractive than a jet black nose against either a blond or a rich golden coat.

The front legs should be straight, with ample – though not coarse and heavy – bone. The feet should turn neither in nor out. The elbows should fit well against the body or the

19

dog will look too wide in front. The feet should be neat and cat-like, with the toes tightly together; splay feet are undesirable as they would not do an effcient job when the dog was working over frozen ground. Similarly, while long, tapering feet are seen, these are also to be avoided. The ideal shape is round.

The 'set' of the tail is the point at which it emerges from the back: it should be level with, and as a natural continuation of, the back. When the dog is moving the tail should never be carried higher than this level. Adolescent males often raise their tails in excitement, but this is temporary and should not be confused with the actual set.

The body of the Golden should never appear skinny and weedy. It is a breed that needs depth at the girth, referred to as 'plenty of heart room'. The ribs should be well sprung, so avoiding any appearance of slab-sidedness. The 'coupling' is the area between where the last rib ends and the hind leg begins, and should be short. The topline should be level: any slope destroys the balanced appearance of the breed, and is frequently found alongside a low-set tail.

The Golden Retriever that moves soundly and well is a joy to watch. His gait should be economical, which is to say he should cover the maximum area with the minimum of effort. It should be a powerful movement, giving the impression that the dog can move all day without tiring. The feet should move in a straight line at both front and back. If the feet converge, they will do so even more at speed, and so trip up the dog and destroy the fluidity of movement. Hackney ponies move with a characteristic 'chopping' stride, and any similarity in a Golden's movement is a fault.

The coat is the Golden's crowning glory. It may be any colour within the range of pale cream to the deepest gold; however, any shade of mahogany or red is a fault. A few white hairs on the chest are allowed. Sometimes white patches are found on top of the head or on the toes, but this is undesirable. The fur should be flat or wavy, or a mixture of both, but never curly. The coat is 'double', with a topcoat and a softer undercoat, the combination of the two giving a water-resistant jacket in wet weather. The longer hair under the tail and belly and on the back of the legs is known as 'feathering', and there should be a good quantity of this, as without it the dog will not look finished.

Puppies will frequently have a white spot on their head, but this should grow out by twelve weeks; the same is true of patches on the toes. All dogs will moult at some time, and will look relatively unattractive until the coat grows again. Large quantities of fluffy undercoat can be combed out, and it is not unusual to fill a carrier bag from a single grooming session.

The ideal height is set out in the standard, and when owners state they want a bitch because she'll be much smaller than a male, they can be right. The height for males is from 56–60cm (22–24in), and for bitches it is 51–56cm (20–22in). The difference between the smallest bitch and the largest dog is marked.

If you wish to show your dog, he will need to have two testicles, descended into the scrotum. A proportion of males retain one or both testicles inside the body cavity. If they do not descend naturally by the time the dog is a year old, they will need to be removed by a veterinary surgeon, as their retention is known to be linked with the development of cancer.

## The Perfect Dog

The standard describes the perfect dog, but we all know that such a dog does not exist. Some come near to it, but every dog has a fault – even the most famous champion dog will have at least one fault, if not more. It is the degree in which that fault exists that is important, remembering the ideal of moderation in all things.

Of course with a young puppy, anyone who stated how closely it fitted the standard would be foolish. If the parents are typical of the breed, then so should be their offspring, but breeding is not always so predictable. Responsible breeders strive to ensure the puppies they produce closely adhere to the standard by only mating sound, typical animals together.

The breed has come a long way from those first retrievers, which were the result of combining several breeds to produce the Golden Retriever as we know it today.

# 2 Finding Your Golden Retriever

Having established that this is the breed for you, the next point to consider is whether you want a puppy or an adult. Each age group has both advantages and disadvantages.

Nothing is quite like the excitement of visiting a breeder to choose your puppy, then watching it grow into a healthy, well adjusted adult. As in all things, however, there is a down side, namely that puppies need round-the-clock attention and make quite a lot of mess. They are easily upset in both the digestive and emotional sense; they also have a huge capacity for chewing, and will not recognize the value of your Chippendale chair as they reduce a leg to splinters.

Purchasing an adult from a breeder is possible, but you will then be taking on a dog that has become used to the ways of others, and you will have missed out on its early development. The purchase price for such an animal can also be high, as the breeder will have borne the costs of rearing and vaccinating it, as well as the hours of time that educating a young dog involves.

Another possibility you might consider is having an unwanted dog. Unbelievably, hundreds of Golden Retrievers are taken into rehoming centres each year, as being no longer required by their owners. They are unwanted for numerous reasons; most commonly their owners have split up or are suffering long-term illness, and in a few cases the owner has died. I have run the Golden Retriever Rescue (Northern Area) for many years, and the number of lovely dogs that come to us is astounding, in all shades and shapes, and of all ages. At least half are well bred and were originally expensive acquisitions, and almost all are Kennel Club registered and vaccinated; moreover they are

*You will need to decide whether you want a puppy or an adult.*

*Rescued dogs make excellent pets for experienced owners.*

frequently insured and are often micro-chipped. It is amazing how readily owners discard these dogs, having initially spent a great deal of money on them.

I would advise only those who have owned a dog before to follow the Rescue route, as these dogs come 'warts and all'. Many have had irresponsible owners who have allowed them to form undesirable habits; it then falls to the new owner to rectify these mistakes, and this is not a task for the novice.

## Where to Find Your Dog

Puppies can be bought in a variety of places, but some of these are a safer bet than others, and whether you are looking for a family pet or a show dog, you will want a healthy puppy, bred from several generations of healthy ancestors.

For many years various health schemes have operated for individual breeds, run by the Kennel Club in conjunction with the British Veterinary Association. Each specific breed is known to be affected by a particular inherited condition, and the tests offered are related to these. Obviously not all dogs from each breed will be affected, but a percentage will, and the only way to stop such conditions being self-perpetuating is never to breed from affected animals or to buy puppies from them.

The inherited conditions of the Golden Retriever are discussed at length elsewhere, but it is relevant to mention them here. This breed, in common with many others, suffers from certain eye defects. Some are instantly obvious, but most are not, and can only be detected by a canine ophthalmic specialist using equipment designed for the purpose. All too often, irresponsible breeders will ask why they should bother having their animals eye-tested when they can apparently see perfectly well. However, although they might appear to see well, because of their highly developed senses of smell and hearing, dogs

*Whether as a pet or for show, a healthy puppy is essential.*

are adept at hiding impaired sight and even blindness. To further complicate the matter, some conditions may be passed on to future generations by dogs that do not appear to have the condition themselves. Such dogs are said to be carriers.

Other problems associated with this breed are elbow dysplasia and hip dysplasia. For these two conditions adult dogs are x-rayed and scored once in their lifetime, and should not be bred from unless they are clear of ED, and fall within an accepted range of scores for HD. The eye test should be done annually throughout a dog's life: some conditions are of late onset, so it would be pointless to test only once or twice. These problems are dealt with in detail in Chapter 8 (*see* page 116).

If the parents of the puppy you are interested in have clearances for the above defects, then the breeder will have current certificates to prove it. Avoid breeders who tell you they don't test their bitches because they always use clear stud dogs. If the bitch has one or more of these defects, then mating her to a clear dog will not prevent some of the puppies being affected.

Avoid at all costs the breeder who is not in possession of the desired paperwork. The schemes are there for the asking, and breeders who do not use them do so for one of two reasons: either they are irresponsible, or they are not prepared to pay the (not inconsiderable) testing fees – at present there is not much change from £200 after paying for hip x-raying and scoring and an annual eye test. Nevertheless, those who breed dogs should do it well, or not at all.

The man-in-the-street who wants to purchase a healthy, well bred puppy faces something of a dilemma. The experienced breeders know who is breeding what, and where they are to be found, and it is this anomaly that leads novice purchasers to reply to newspaper advertisements offering puppies for sale. Breeders advertising in this way will, in the

main, be pet breeders, and not all will test their animals for inherited problems. There will also be a few who do absolutely everything right but who are just not aware of where or how to advertise. For those breeding in a responsible way, the best route for advertising is through the many Golden Retriever clubs, because they only accept litters from hip-scored and eye-tested parents. The tests never guarantee that each puppy is clear of undesirable traits, but they will lessen the chances.

The Kennel Club now offers breeders the chance to advertise litters through their organization. A fee is paid, and details of the litter are forwarded to those who contact the Kennel Club in search of a puppy. Buyers must be aware that this list is comprised of puppies registered with the Kennel Club, and whose owners have paid a fee. It is not a vetted list, so it is vital that you do your own checks if you wish to purchase in this way.

Many reputable breeders have websites – but so do the unscrupulous. Be wary of those who offer several breeds for sale, as they could be the dreaded 'puppy farmers'. These are breeders whose sole objective is to make

*Breed clubs will only promote litters from healthy parents.*

as much profit as possible, irrespective of the welfare of their charges. Such establishments may be overcrowded, unhygienic and frequently disease-ridden; some sound superb, but the reality is vastly different. If you find yourself at such an unsavoury establishment, walk away, and *do not* fall into the trap of purchasing because you feel sorry for the puppy; by so doing you will be encouraging the breeding of more litters, and may be sold a sub-standard pup, leading to heartache and great expense.

Other places to avoid are the smart-looking establishments resembling supermarkets that sell puppies, kittens, rabbits and other small furry creatures, as well as pet food and accessories. I took in such a puppy last year to save it from being destroyed when the student owner, who had been keeping it as a pet on the top floor of her university hall of residence, returned to China. In her defence, she kept the puppy immaculately and it was fed and reared well, but she should never have had a dog in the first place. She had a very understanding professor, who allowed the dog to attend lectures – but keeping any dog in this way is far from ideal. This puppy was advertised as 'registered', implying Kennel Club registration. The documents were impressive, gold-lettered on a maroon background, but the body with which the dog was supposedly registered did not exist. Furthermore the price paid for this puppy was at the top end of what a reputable show kennel would charge. Such establishments should not be supported, because once the young animals are past the fluffy, appealing stage, they are very often destroyed – and everyone who buys from such places helps to perpetuate this cruel practice.

Another way of finding a puppy is to scan the 'For Sale' columns of the various dog magazines. There are weekly papers devoted to all things canine, and there are also glossy monthly magazines offering the same. Most who advertise in these are serious breeders – but not all, so proceed with caution and check out your chosen breeder thoroughly.

There is no completely foolproof way of ensuring you have found a reputable breeder, but generally if they keep a few healthy, happy-looking Goldens with current certificates and other relevant paperwork, you are part of the way to ensuring you have not inadvertently gone to a puppy farmer.

Another way to ensure that a breeder is not overbreeding his bitches, is by checking the number of litters being produced in the Kennel Club's publication, *The Breed Records Supplement*. This is published quarterly and is available by subscription. A few hours spent reading this will often tell you more than talking to many breeders.

## The Breed Clubs

There are many clubs devoted to the Golden Retriever, and most areas of the British Isles have at least one local one, or more. In Yorkshire we have the Yorkshire Golden Retriever Club, but the county is also served by the Northern Golden Retriever Association. Most of these clubs offer a facility whereby, for a fee, members can advertise litters on their web site – but only litters from hip-scored, eye-tested parents qualify to go on to these sites. Secretaries of the various clubs are usually very knowledgeable about the breed, and will be able to answer most of the novice owner's questions.

Narrow your choice of breeder down to a maximum of three, then ask if you can visit. Be honest, and tell each one that you are visiting others before making your choice. While there will always be a few who will see that as a chance to denigrate the kennels of others, the honest breeder will respect you for taking adequate care.

Be reasonable about how many of you visit. I once had a coachload of Canadians who only asked if they could visit when they rang

*Be reasonable regarding how many visit when choosing a puppy.*

from the phone on the village green! Usually it is the extended family who wants to come, including parents, grandparents and children. However, in the first instance it is most productive if just the parents visit, because then there are no distractions and the conversation can proceed without the interruptions of over-excited children. Also, the more people present, the more excited dogs tend to be. You want visitors to see your dogs at their best, not as a hyper-active pack that presses them to the wall, licking their faces vigorously!

Try not to request a visit at odd hours. Kennel owners are busy all day, and it is irritating when, having done all the jobs and settled down for the evening, visitors arrive. Avoid early morning visits because breeders will be busy then; generally, early afternoon is the best time for most people. It is useful to ask at what time the puppies are fed, because if you visit immediately after they've had a meal, they will all be asleep and you'll see very little.

I would recommend visiting breeders when they haven't got litters. Go just to talk to them and to see their adult dogs. This gives you longer to consider if this is the breeder for you, rather than being presented with a litter about which you feel pressurized to make a decision in case all sell quickly.

Most good breeders are well booked for future litters, and may have many bookings before the bitch is mated. I am in that position

*Visit before the litter is fed or they will be sleepy.*

now, and because I want to keep back a puppy for myself, must ensure that I don't accept more bookings than there will be puppies. Some breeders ask for a deposit when a potential buyer books a puppy. I never do, as I like to give buyers an escape route whereby they can change their minds if necessary, rather than feeling they have to go ahead because they've paid.

## What to Look For

Having narrowed your choice to three kennels, it is important to know what you are looking for before you visit. Make a list, as the excitement of the moment is likely to drive away all questions you had intended to ask.

First impressions are important. If the breeder hurries to put dogs out of the way when you arrive, ask yourself why she does this. Are they too aggressive or shy for the visitor to meet them? Is their condition poor and she doesn't want you to see them? Be suspicious if you are severely restricted as to where you are allowed to go. Are all areas closed to you except one? Why is this?

Do not confuse being excluded from some areas with an ulterior motive, as the responsible breeder will be worried about the many feet of your family potentially treading in infection to unvaccinated puppies. Do not take offence if she asks you to remove your shoes or sprays their soles. You should also expect to wash your hands before touching puppies, as they are very vulnerable.

The smell of a breeding establishment speaks volumes. If it is run well, on clean and hygienic lines, there should be no unpleasant odour. Neither should the adult dogs smell. There will always be the isolated incident where you arrive just as one of the dogs has rolled in something unsavoury, but in general, they should be clean and sweet-smelling. Luckily, the Golden is not a breed

*Watch how the breeder interacts with the dogs.*

that has a strong body odour, unlike some breeds that smell like wet woolly sweaters.

Watch the way the breeder deals with the puppies and adults. Is she gentle and obviously fond of them, or cold and distant towards them? How do the dogs react to her? If they are subservient and cringe, then she is probably not very kind to them when you are not there.

Look at her dog-food store: is it clean and well kept? This is one way you can see if the puppies are actually fed on what her diet sheet tells you they eat.

All this seems rather 'cloak and dagger', but nothing could be worse than getting home with your puppy only to find everything wrong, and then to learn just how undesirable your breeder is.

If you are able to meet others who have bought a puppy from this breeder in the past, so much the better. You will learn a great deal from those who already have her puppies, and if she hasn't played fairly with them, then she will probably not play fair with you, either. Equally, if you do not care for the look of their puppy now that it has grown, you might feel the same way about yours.

The puppy you will choose is a commitment that may last for fifteen years, so it is important that you choose wisely and well.

## How to Choose Your Puppy

It is useful just to watch the whole litter playing. By observing them in this way it will become instantly obvious which one is the leader, which is the quietest, and if there are any shy puppies – although it is by no means certain that the characteristics they exhibit now will persist throughout their lives.

Watch how they interact with their breeder and with their dam. Observe how they react to loud or unusual noises. It is natural for all puppies to jump when they hear a loud noise, but those that are well adjusted should regain their composure on realizing that no harm will come to them.

I accustom my puppies to standing on a table to be examined from the time they are five weeks old. It is very diffcult for the potential buyer if the first time they see the puppies is also the first time these are expected to stand on a table. From the breeder's point of view, the first time you attempt to stand the puppy on a table (with a non-slip mat placed on it) it is unlikely that he will stand still: usually he will wriggle and struggle, and even try to jump off. Support him under the chin, and it helps to have a tasty treat in one hand for him to nibble at as he stands. Great care is needed to ensure he does not jump off, or injury could result. By the tenth time you practise this exercise, the puppy usually

*Observe if there are any shy puppies in the litter.*

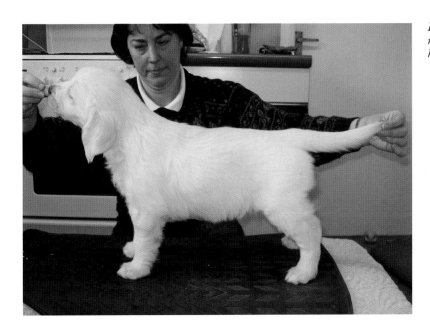

*I liked this puppy so much that she came home with me.*

understands what you want him to do. Actually getting strangers to examine him is entirely different, and usually all your good training dissolves into hilarity as breeder and owner-to-be attempt to keep him on the table!

The eight-week-old puppy should appear nicely rounded without being overweight. He should have chunky legs and bright, clean eyes, with no sign of discharge. Remember that the eyes of young puppies are blue, and the desired dark brown colour is not obvious until twelve weeks or later. Furthermore the depth of blue has no bearing at all on how dark the eventual brown will be.

The puppy's fur should be clear and free from dandruff, and his skin should be clean and pale. Reddened areas are indicative of irritation, and places to examine include behind the ears, between the forelegs and on the belly; inside the hind legs is a favourite site for eczema or parasitic infection. The skin should be loose and pliable: a tight-skinned puppy is a dehydrated one. Ask the breeder to gently lift a fold of skin to show that there is

looseness. Run your fingers against the way the coat lies naturally: if your nails come into contact with what feels like large grains of sand, these will be scabs left over from a parasitic infection.

At this stage, it is very diffcult to assess whether the puppy has the correct bite as the

*The puppy should be well grown.*

29

teeth are so tiny and will change to adult teeth very soon. If the lower jaw appears to project in front of the upper, then it is likely that as an adult the dog will have a faulty jaw.

As the puppies run about, their legs should move freely with no 'bulldog'-type fronts. The limbs should be straight and fit well against the body.

## Dog or Bitch

If you ask advice from owners regarding whether dogs or bitches make better pets, they will almost certainly be divided. Often, those who have only ever owned one sex will speak in a derogatory manner about the other. After more than forty years of owning both, I can honestly say I like both equally. The males have a sense of humour and can be clowns, loving to 'play to the gallery'. They are bigger and stronger, and are also heavier than bitches. They tend to moult less, but their coats are heavier and take more grooming; they also take longer to dry after a bath.

A few Goldens might not care for other males, but these are in the minority, and it is generally dogs that have been kept in isolation instead of being well socialized when young, that exhibit this behaviour.

If your neighbours have bitches and your gardens adjoin, your male can be a problem when they are in season. Such behaviour could include digging to get at them, constant barking or howling, and nearly always a

*You will need to decide whether you prefer a dog or a bitch.*

*Golden Retriever puppies are irresistible.*

*Puppies spend a great deal of time sleeping.*

### To Neuter or Not

Vets are very quick to suggest that we have dogs neutered, putting forward the argument that it will prevent them from developing testicular cancer later in life. While this is a worthwhile consideration, a recent detailed study by Laura Sanbam, published in March 2007, presents some worrying side-effects of neutering and spaying. For example, spaying bitches shows an increase in osteosarcoma when done before maturity, and causes urinary incontinence in up to twenty per cent of bitches. The risk of vaginal dermatitis, vaginitis and recurring vaginal infections increases with bitches spayed before puberty, while arguments rage regarding spaying as a contributing factor to adverse reactions to vaccinations. Male dogs who are neutered while immature also have an increased risk of osteosarcoma and an increased risk of geriatric cognitive impairment (doggy Alzheimers). As with bitches, they are believed to show increased risk of adverse reaction to vaccinations.

non-stop session of urinating on plants and fences.

Bitches have the great disadvantage of coming into season, when they attract male dogs and disrupt holidays. They are sweet and considerably smaller than the dogs. It is a fallacy that they will roam less than males because all dogs, irrespective of their gender, will wander if the gate is left open.

Bitches moult more frequently and tend to put on weight more easily in the middle years – though weight gain is not diffcult to control, as so many reduced calorie diets now exist. My bitches have always been considerably greedier than my males, and never appear full after a meal. A friend describes them as 'jaws on paws', which is appropriate.

The choice between dogs and bitches is purely personal. In general, owners from families where there have only ever been bitches, in their turn tend to choose to own bitches. Many myths surround males, and these play no small part in influencing the owners' choice.

## Choosing Your Puppy

It is a good idea to choose the puppy you prefer in advance of eight weeks of age; when you go back again when it is time to collect, you must hope you still like the same one. Breeders generally mark each puppy by cutting off a piece of fur and recording in a book whose puppy it is. So, my present puppy would say 'Anderson. Left hind leg'. Some breeders use felt-tip pen or nail varnish to mark puppies, but my experience has been that both substances disappear rather quickly.

If you do not like the puppy at eight weeks that you raved over at six weeks, it is vitally important that you say so, or you will leave with a dog you are disappointed in, which is hardly the way to begin a partnership that could span fifteen years.

Sometimes there will be a 'spare' puppy that has not yet been chosen, and the breeder will offer you that. It is more likely, however, that all will have been chosen, so you must be honest and say that you have decided that it is not the puppy for you. The breeder will not be too pleased, but, on the other hand, should be relieved that you changed your mind before taking it home.

## Collecting Your Puppy

Discuss diet with the breeder before you actually collect the puppy, so that you can have exactly the right food bought in advance. At the time of collection expect to be given a diet sheet. If this is not forthcoming, ask for instructions and make notes, because you will never recall all you have been told on reaching home. The registration certificate for your puppy will be given to you, and you should be shown the section you have to fill in to transfer him into your name.

Many breeders have a first vaccination for all the puppies before they go, so ensure you have the certificate for this, as you will need to hand it to your vet to enable him to complete the second vaccination. The pedigree will also be given to you. This may come in the form of a hand-written one, or one produced on a computer, or it may be the offcial Kennel Club one. All these types are equally correct. I have a preference for hand-written ones (which, as this electronic age advances, are becoming rarer) as they have a personal element that is lacking in the others. If you are given one written by the breeder or produced on a computer, you may pay for the Kennel Club's offcial one at a later date.

First-time owners sometimes like to frame these. Armed with these documents and your new puppy, you can now begin your life together.

## Travelling Home

It is important that the puppy feels secure as he leaves the familiarity of his house for the rather scary world of cars. I like to have him on my lap, but if you are driving alone, he will need a carrying box. Even if you have a dog-guard in the rear of your car, there will be too much space for him and he will be thrown about as you brake and corner, in a way that could frighten him and thereby imprint in him a fear of travelling for life.

The travelling box should have a piece of non-slip bedding inside, and should be large enough for him to stand, sit and turn around in, but not so large that he can get thrown about. I always place the box in the well of the passenger seat, so that the puppy can see me. If it's a sunny day, ensure that he is shaded and that the air conditioning is on. He will possibly be sick, and some puppies evacuate both bowel and bladder.

Take a survival kit with you so that you can change the soiled bedding, and a plastic bag to put it in. Also have a water dish and water. Fill your water bottle from the breeder's tap as water differs widely according to its place of origin, and this will ensure he is not upset. Large wet-wipes, such as are used for babies, are useful if the puppy's fur becomes soiled. It is a very unpleasant experience for both owner and puppy if the bedding cannot be changed en route.

Most puppies will fall asleep after a short time, and will only wake on reaching their destination. There is always the exception to the rule, however, and the owners of these puppies will regale those willing to listen with accounts of how they kept up a constant yapping from breeder to new home. But such

*When travelling, puppies will experience too much movement if the space is too large.*

instances are rare, and if the puppy behaves like that, there is absolutely nothing you can do about it. Sometimes turning on the car radio will stop a puppy from making a noise. I know someone who always plays a CD of sounds designed to calm the listener, and she is convinced it helps. There are also plug-in devices that emit calming pheromones, the same as those used to calm dogs fearful of fireworks.

## Children and Dogs

Children and dogs are a good partnership, as each teaches the other a sense of responsibility. It is well known that children who are diffcult will often be perfectly well adjusted with their dog companion.

Every time a child is bitten by a dog, the media coverage is extensive – but those who understand dogs will immediately ask what the child was doing, that caused the dog to bite. In many households dogs will tolerate treatment from children which they would not put up with from adults, and appear to have a built-in sense of needing to be more forgiving of youngsters.

This tolerance should never be abused, and it is vitally important that any interaction between dogs and children is supervised by responsible adults. The breed is renowned for its good nature, but even the best-tempered dogs have a zero-tolerance zone. In common with a pain threshold, this differs within individual dogs.

Children must be taught how to handle small puppies, and should be encouraged to sit on the floor before picking them up. Puppies, like small babies, can suddenly throw themselves about, which could result in injury and even tragedy if the child were standing or sitting on a chair.

A puppy needs supporting under its forelegs and bottom, and will struggle as a result of feeling insecure if not held firmly and safely. Puppies that cling on for dear life, digging in their claws, are feeling anxious about being held.

*The delight on this child's face is obvious.*

*This puppy would be safer if his young owner were seated.*

All puppies chew fingers, toes, shoes and the hems of trousers and skirts. Woolly sweaters are irresistible to their teeth and claws, which become entangled and must be extricated gently. Children must learn the critical difference between a puppy that mouths playfully, and one that bites.

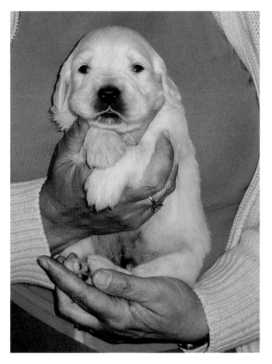

*Puppies must feel secure when being held.*

Mouthing is a characteristic of the Golden Retriever, in common with other gundogs, and he will hold on to wrists and fingers, and will attempt to 'lead' visitors around. This should never be viewed as aggression: it is merely an essential component of the gundog's need to carry. Sadly, several Goldens that exhibit this trait are brought into Rescue each year because their owners fear that such behaviour is the forerunner of viciousness. But nothing could be further from the truth, and the habit is viewed by those who understand the breed as endearing.

I have never sold my puppies to people with very young children as I believe parents have plenty to do with young families without the added work that having a puppy involves. Puppies are also extremely breakable, and a small child falling could result in disaster. Neither do I allow my Rescue dogs to go to homes with young children, because if they have come from an adults-only environment, they might not be tolerant of youngsters.

Children and dogs that deal with each other with respect and understanding derive mutual enjoyment from the partnership and have their lives greatly enriched.

# 3  The First Year

*Bad habits are difficult to break.*

*Areas to which puppies have access must be secure.*

This will be the most challenging, exciting, and sometimes exasperating time for you and your dog. At this stage, how you train him is crucial, as lessons learned are extremely difficult for the dog to unlearn. Similarly, bad habits formed at this stage will last for a very long time.

## Toilet Training

Once you arrive home with your puppy, the first thing you will want him to learn is that he empties his bowels and bladder outdoors, and not in the house. If he was reared in an outdoor kennel or had access to an outdoor run, then you are halfway there. Puppies reared exclusively in the home take longer to train.

Puppies have the urge to relieve themselves on waking and as soon as they finish eating. Your task is to be swift without scaring the puppy, because initially you need to carry him outside before he realizes he needs to go. Praise enthusiastically when he delivers. Take care where you persuade him to perform, because once he considers that particular place as his toilet area, he will return to it.

Owners employ various methods to encourage puppies to perform. Some construct a small sandpit, others will make a gravelled square within a concreted area. Grass is a favourite, but is diffcult to keep clean. If you are reserving a section of your lawn, be aware that it will turn yellow (particularly from bitch's urine), and will be impossible to restore to its former green.

If the puppy has been encouraged to use newspaper as a toilet area while still with his breeder, then it will aid training if you continue to put down paper. Placing a thick newspaper near the back door is a good idea, as it is here that most accidents are likely to happen.

## At Night

Your puppy will need a bed, a drink and paper as a toileting area when you leave him for the night. Ideally the newspaper should be placed far enough away from the bed to prevent any leakages wetting it. The water dish (heavy enough to be neither thrown about nor carried) also needs to be distant from the bed and paper, otherwise a soggy mess will result.

Ensure that the area where the puppy is left is absolutely safe. It is amazing just how small a space a puppy can crawl into, and should that space contain electric leads, the result could be fatal.

Take equal care that the puppy does not have access to cupboards where cleaning materials are stored: the kitchen and bathroom contain as many toxic preparations as the garden shed. Dishwasher powder is lethal, and the smallest amount can cause death. Fit childproof locks on unit doors as a safeguard.

Some puppies chew, so if your kitchen or utility room, which you have destined to double as a canine nursery, sports designer fittings, you might have to think again. I deplore the use of cages or crates as dog housing, and believe more dogs live in utter misery as a result of the popularity of these 'prisons' than most other causes. By far preferable is the heavy duty puppy pen, which can be purchased as individual panels that link together. As the puppy grows, you can add panels, and as this structure is portable, it can be erected in the garden so that the puppy is with you but safe from harmful plants. These playpens permit a far greater degree of freedom than cages, and are far more robust.

Do not expect house training to happen overnight, as puppies consume large quantities of liquid but have very small bladders. Most will produce three or four puddles of urine overnight, and during the day they will seldom last an hour without needing to relieve themselves.

*When left at night, ensure the puppy is safe.*

**Dealing with Suspected Cystitis**

Be watchful for the puppy that squats frequently, sometimes as often as every minute, and then takes a while standing up: it is possible he has cystitis (*see* Chapter 8). This is extremely painful, and needs instant veterinary attention. If you do suspect your puppy might have this problem, take him to the vet, together with a urine sample; the latter will give a speedy diagnosis.

To collect a urine sample requires speed and a degree of ingenuity! Slide a clean jam-jar lid between the puppy and the floor as he squats; then tip the urine into the clean jar, and this can then be transported to the vet's surgery.

Your male puppy will not cock his leg for several months, and some may reach a year old before they do it. Owners feel a ridiculous sense of pride on the first occasion their puppy aims high! Males that live with bitches have been known to squat in the manner of their companions throughout life. There is nothing wrong with males that do this.

## Feeding

When a puppy arrives at his new home he will be too excited, or too queasy from the journey, to eat. Give him several hours before you offer him a meal, but ensure fresh water is always accessible. Do not be alarmed if he doesn't eat well the first day you have him, as there is much to distract him as well as the strangeness of new surroundings. Most are ready to eat by the next morning.

Do adhere absolutely to the breeder's diet sheet. To alter the food the puppy is accustomed to, will almost certainly cause him to have a bout of diarrhoea. Furthermore, if you have visitors, and particularly children, ensure they do not feed him human food. While the giving of sensible titbits is used as a reward for good behaviour or to strengthen the bond between owner and puppy, the wrong titbits can have undesirable, and in some cases even lethal, results.

Although you will be closely following the breeder's instructions for feeding your puppy, the quantities will need to be increased. It's safe to assume that if the puppy looks good, is gaining weight steadily, and appears satisfied, then you have got it right.

However well the puppy has eaten while one of a group, it is fairly normal for him to decide he is not so interested in food once he is alone in his new home. Usually this indifference lasts just for a day or two, but there will always be the occasional puppy that stops eating or just picks at his food. The urge to buy anything that might start him eating again is best avoided or he (and you) will play the food-refusal game indefinitely. Put the food down without any fuss, allow five minutes for him to eat, then remove what remains. Resist the temptation to look at him every few minutes to see if he has eaten it; if he hasn't, he will come to no harm until the next mealtime, as long as he has ample fresh water available.

It is unfortunate that soon after puppies go to their new homes is a time that coincides with their milk teeth falling out, and their permanent set coming through. Inevitably their mouths are very sore throughout this period; sometimes soaking the food that the puppy has normally enjoyed dry, will start him eating again.

If after several days food is offered but is still being refused, then it really is time to try something else. There are now good quality gravy products made just for puppies, and usually a squirt of that on the usual food works wonders. If you decide to change the food he is used to, do it gradually, with a percentage of his usual food and a percentage of the new variety. Avoid any sudden changes, as this is guaranteed to upset a puppy's digestive system.

*Puppies eat better when they have competition.*

## Foods to Avoid

There are some foods that are extremely harmful to dogs. Grapes, raisins and sultanas cause kidney failure, and it is not possible to predict a 'safe' quantity for these foods, as dogs have died as a result of eating as little as a few grapes, or as much as a large bunch. We can all recite stories of dogs that regularly eat grapes and their dried cousins with no ill effect, but for every dog who eats them and does not become ill, there will be many more that die as a result of eating comparatively few. The danger lies in the fact that the 'safe' quantity does not exist, and what is tolerated by some would be fatal for others.

Dogs must not be fed chocolate, onions (or any member of the onion family) or Macadamia nuts. Another highly toxic substance is the cocoa-shell mulch that is sold for the garden: it is irresistible to dogs as it smells like drinking chocolate, but even a small quantity can be fatal.

While no one would feed pot pourri to dogs, they are greatly attracted to it, particularly the vanilla-scented variety, and it is highly toxic. One problem with pot pourri is that much of it is very fine, and pieces will be blown up and about the room in the draught of doors being open and closed, and thereby it becomes accessible to dogs. If you must have this product in your house, place it in a container with a lid, on a high shelf.

## What Else Could Harm the Puppy?

Be very cautious about using any of the products marketed as able to 'hide' or 'remove' household odours. An advertisement for one such product shows the woman of the house liberally spraying the dog's bed: but consider how sensitive a dog's nose is, and imagine how irritating (if not dangerous) such a chemical could be.

Ensure that floor cleaners are used in the correct dilution. Dogs walk on floors, then lick their paws, thereby transferring some of the chemicals to their mouth.

I am obsessive about bleach. The only safe place to use it is in the toilet bowl, with the lid

39

*Goldens are besotted with water.*

firmly in place – remember that many dogs like to drink from the toilet. I regularly see kennel owners cleaning runs with hot water and bleach, and all assure me it is a way of controlling disease. That's as maybe, but bleach takes a massive amount of rinsing before there is no trace left. It burns and destroys the pads and has disastrous results if it gets into the eyes. The only safe bleach is the bleach still in its sealed container, which is never used near dogs.

The same caution is needed when using some of the virucides. Years ago, one was marketed as being so safe that drinking bowls could be cleaned with it – but not so long after, it was found to have cancer-causing properties.

Dogs are not too fond of highly scented fabric conditioners, but while they are not harmful as such, they are better avoided.

Several preparations are available that clean carpets by being shaken on to the pile, and then vacuumed out. Many instances of dogs developing allergies were recorded after lying on carpets treated in this way.

Perhaps the most dangerous substance of all is anti-freeze, as its sweetness makes it attractive to dogs, with fatal results.

## The Garden

Your dog will need to play in the garden, but it is not always a safe area. We live in an age when electrically operated garden features are common, but unless the cables are armoured the puppy could easily chew through to the live core.

Ponds have caused the death of many puppies, because if they fall in and the sides are steep, they quickly become exhausted trying in vain to climb out, with fatal results. Either cover the pond, or keep your puppy out of the area altogether. All Goldens are quite besotted with water, so the need to keep the dog away from the pond will remain throughout his life.

Canes used to support plants should be the sort with fixed, rounded tops. If you have canes with removable tops, the latter will be speedily removed and swallowed, and the exposed tops of canes are dangerous for both human and canine eyes.

Some of the most beautiful and inoffensive-looking plants are poisonous to dogs. Foxgloves (*digitalis*) cause coma and death. The rhododendron and azalea family are poisonous, as are lupins, daffodils and crocus. Laurel contains acid, which is a certain killer:

*All parts of the foxglove are deadly.*

*The leaves and berries of laurel are poisonous.*

we once lost a Friesian cow within hours of it snatching a mouthful of leaves. Other poisonous plants include autumn crocus, lily of the valley, broom (all parts are fatal), daphne, delphinium, gloriosa lily, laburnum, lantana and yew.

Two plants which do not grow in our climate must be mentioned, because their seeds are imported as jewellery or rosary beads. The first is the castor bean (*Ricinus communis*), whose mottled seeds make attractive necklaces and rosary beads, which are frequently brought into Britain as souvenirs; these contain ricin, one of the deadliest poisons – a single seed would kill a grown man. The second, and even more attractive, is the rosary pea (*Abrus precatorius*). These highly polished, pea-shaped seeds are scarlet with a jet black spot at one end, and contain a lethal cocktail of poisons. They are used for necklaces, rosaries and dolls' eyes, and are so uniform in size that they were used by goldsmiths for weighing precious metals.

To be absolutely safe, never allow puppies or grown dogs to have access to any seed

*Low-growing ivy is easily accessible, but is poisonous.*    *A small quantity of yew will cause death.*

*The attractive variegated ivy is just as harmful as its common relative.*

*All parts of the lovely golden form of yew are poisonous.*

jewellery: while not all contain deadly poisons, others contain toxins that would cause extreme sickness and allergic reactions. Many such necklaces look just like stones, but it is often their lack of weight when compared with the real article which gives a clue as to their plant origin.

## Toys

There are so many toys available now that it is diffcult to choose a selection for the new puppy. Basically, he needs something to chew on and something to carry. Toys for chewing need to be extremely robust, or small pieces will be chewed off. I prefer to give my puppies the white, chalky, sterilized bones often sold as 'calcium bones'; these do not shatter like most bones, and the chalky deposit which results from chewing will do no harm.

There are specially treated rubber toys available which are guaranteed to withstand even the most enthusiastic chewers. I always go for the sizes recommended for larger breeds, as such toys become more impervious to chewing as they move up the size scale.

*Toys for chewing must be robust.*

*Balls with concealed treats will entertain puppies for hours.*

There are plastic cubes and balls available in which small treats can be concealed; as the puppy noses these around the floor, treats will be dispensed randomly. Such toys should be used under supervision, as I have never found one that is chew-proof. For younger puppies which do not have great strength in their jaws, such toys are ideal, but older pups soon become frustrated when the treats refuse to appear as fast as they would like, and soon work out that the way to get *all* the treats is to chew a hole in the dispenser!

Soft, furry toys are loved by Goldens. Some will keep the same toy for years, while others will 'disembowel' it instantly. A good damage-limitation ploy is to select a toy with the least number of chewable peaks. A furry dog with floppy ears and long tail would be a prime candidate for demolition. The toy that lasts longest for my dogs is a large, furry banana because there are no extraneous parts to stand on and pull off!

Knotted rope toys have a mixed following. Some breeders always use them with no undesired results, others tell tales of bunches of fibres breaking off and wrapping around the puppy's tongue. Some have had to be removed from puppies' stomachs. I allow my puppies to play at carrying and shaking them, but once they settle to a serious chewing session, the toys are temporarily removed.

Hide chews are sold in all sorts of weird and wonderful shapes, from flat strips to intricate knots. When these first came on to the market, many owners saw them as the answer to stopping their dogs chewing the furniture. Many bought the very large knotted chews that would keep the dog occupied for hours. Most dogs chew these with no ill effects, but every so often a case is reported to the contrary; a famous show dog died as a result of a very large chewed-off lump lodging in his intestines. I allow young puppies (from 8–12 weeks) to chew such toys as I watch them, but once these objects start to

Unlike a ball, these toys bounce erratically, so the puppy derives great fun from never knowing in which direction his toy will go.

Balls are dangerous if they are small enough to stick in the throat, especially if they are made of solid rubber. A saliva-soiled ball, stuck at the back of the mouth, will block the dog's airway and is virtually impossible to remove. If you must have a ball for the puppy, make it a tennis ball or a small, soft football. While the puppy will not be able to carry the latter, he will have hours of fun nosing it around.

Sticks must never be thrown for dogs. At best they wedge across the dog's upper jaw or, when the dog jumps to catch it, can perforate the soft palate when he lands, or do inoperable damage deeper in the throat. A splendid toy has just come on to the market in the form of a soft rubber branch. This is definitely a carrying toy, and not one that can be left with the puppy to chew. Older dogs, whose joints are fully formed, can have great fun fetching this toy when it is thrown.

become soft – and it is at this point that quite large pieces break off and can be swallowed – I remove them. They will dry and harden off, so can be given back to the puppy for a supervised chewing session the following day.

## Lead Training

The earlier the puppy is introduced to a collar and lead the better, as once his vaccinations have been completed, he will need to go out and meet the world. To begin his training, the puppy should wear a soft collar around the house. Take this off when you cannot supervise him, as collars can get caught up on a variety of things in the house and garden.

There are as many different types of collar and lead available as there are breeds of dog.

*Patience is needed for puppies to accept a collar and lead.*

The selection of these items is a matter of personal choice, but the puppy should have a lightweight collar and lead, strong enough to withstand pulling. My preferred style is the webbing collars and leads: they are light, durable and can be washed, and they are also extremely strong. They are not impervious to chewing, but neither is leather.

The metal choke chain is barbaric and should be banned. If you are in any doubt, place one around your wrist and give a sharp tug; then imagine that around your throat, for that is what the poor dog wearing one will feel. A retractable lead is a useful training aid, but for general walking I find them heavy and cumbersome, and there have been far too many reports of them snapping when the dog races to their full extent.

The collar must be tight enough for the puppy not to be able to pull his head through, but loose enough to be comfortable. Generally if you can place two fingers between the collar and neck, then it is the right size.

Some pups take to lead training without any objections, and others will roll over and fight in an attempt to rid themselves of both collar and lead. Patience and titbits usually work wonders. As the puppy takes his first few steps while wearing his collar and lead, walk backwards so he is coming towards you, encouraging him all the time, and reward him with treats at intervals. At first, two 5min sessions a day are all that is required; if you do more, the puppy will become tired of the lesson and will look for distractions. The whole object of such lessons is to make them fun and rewarding.

## Basic Command Training

The lessons that may be taught from eight weeks onwards are sitting, staying, lying down, and the recall.

## The Sit

The puppy should be on your left side, wearing a collar with lead attached. Say 'Sit', and at the same time gently push down on his rump with your left hand while simultaneously raising the lead with your right hand, so causing the puppy to look up.

Repeat the procedure up to six times at each training session, and very soon your puppy will realize what is required of him. Praise enthusiastically when he complies. Remember, with this and all exercises, there needs to be an obvious point where the dog is no longer under command. One idea is to praise the puppy for sitting, then give another command to mark the end, such as 'Off you go', or 'Run away', stepping forward to encourage the dog out of a sitting position as you do so.

Puppies learn this exercise so quickly that before you know it they will be sitting if you so much as look as if you are going to give the order!

## The Stay

I use 'Wait' as a command in preference to 'Stay', as bright pups hear the letter 's' that begins both 'Sit' and 'Stay', and may be confused over which was the intended command. This was something I learned initially with Border Collies, who are extremely intelligent and who anticipate every word their handler utters. It is a good idea to have the puppy feeling really confident about the 'Sit' and the 'Down' before starting to teach the 'Stay'.

Give the command 'Wait' when the dog is either in a lying or sitting position, and as you do so put your left hand in front of his muzzle, palm facing the dog. Every puppy wants to follow his owner, and every contact he will have had with you so far will have been connected with his closeness to you. But suddenly you now want him to distance himself from you, and, even more confusing, you are praising him for doing so.

Much patience is needed for this exercise on both the dog and the handler's part, and it is very much a case of making haste slowly. A useful ploy is to perform this exercise near a post or slender tree, round which the lead can be looped, running freely. If the puppy attempts to follow, a tug on the lead will dissuade him.

All exercises are important, but this is the one that could save your dog's life. Imagine the scenario where he is racing towards a gate, inadvertently left open, which leads on to a busy road. His reaction to your 'Wait' could avert an accident.

## The Down

Kneel beside your dog when he is in a sitting position, and give the command 'Down'. Gently move your hand under his paws to bring him into a lying position – the earlier you start this exercise, the lighter the puppy will be to manoeuvre into position. Once he assumes the correct position, keep him there with your left hand applying light pressure over his shoulders, and use the command 'Down. Stay'. Some puppies panic a little when you first move their paws, and it is essential that all is done in a calm and gentle manner.

### Rewards

All that most Goldens require as a reward for good behaviour is the sound of their owner's voice, praising them. Sometimes treats may be used to obtain the desired result, but use them sparingly as a treat should be just that, and not *always* available. It is helpful to use treats that are dry and pleasant to handle. I use the small biscuits that comprise a complete diet for cats.

## The Recall

Have the puppy sitting in front of you, step backwards and, as you do so, tug the lead and say 'Come'. To add variety to this, you can step straight back and give the command, or step to the right or left. Praise enthusiastically when he obeys. To start with you will be retreating just one or two steps before giving the 'Come' command; then progress to the length of the lead. Before long you will be able to go to the full length of the longest retractable lead.

## Points to Ponder

- Remember, when you commence training your dog you will have a great advantage over him because although *you* know what he is expected to do, *he* has no idea.
- Dogs learn at different rates, and just because another Golden of the same age masters the 'Sit' in one session, it does not mean that your dog will learn as fast. Speed of learning is no indication as to how reliable at that exercise the dog will eventually be.
- Calmness and kindness are essential. We are all human, and few of us have not experienced a moment where we could easily lose our tempers. Should you do so, you will have taken a retrograde step that will take many months to undo.
- Be aware that your dog only hears the tone of words. To praise in a gruff, loud voice is conveyed to the dog as a scolding. Listen to the top obedience competitors who know just how to keep it light and fun.
- If training becomes a chore for you and the dog, you are missing the point.
- Training takes time, and your lessons, given in short, easy-to-assimilate chunks, will not be learned overnight. Even the top obedience competitors at Crufts only get to, and maintain their level by practice and reward over a considerable length of time.

## Other Exercises

Once your puppy has mastered the basics of training, the opportunities of furthering his education are endless. He can be trained to go away from you to a marked spot as the 'Send Away'; or he can find an article with your scent on it as 'Scent Discrimination'. He can be taught to jump – although this should not be allowed until he is fully mature and you have had his hips x-rayed to see if he is physically sound enough for this exercise.

Other ways of having fun with your dog are covered in Chapter 7 (page 100) where we look at the varied opportunities available to dog and handler.

## Socialization

Of all the things you do with your puppy, socializing is the most important as he will never be able to live comfortably in the world unless he accepts it with all its noise, bustle and surprise. You cannot start socializing too early, and it is a great hindrance that puppies are not able to go to public places until all vaccinations are completed. However, this does not mean you should sit around, leaving the puppy to his own devices until twelve weeks of age.

During this time he should be subjected to all normal household noises, such as the vacuum cleaner, the washing machine, television and radio. It is now possible to buy recordings of noises so that pups may become accustomed to them; these include the sounds of fireworks, vehicles, machinery, crowds and much more. During his 'isolation' time there is no reason why he cannot go for car rides. He should travel in a safe manner, such as in a travelling crate or behind a guard in your car (although the latter method often provides too much space, allowing him to be thrown around as you corner or brake).

*Most veterinary practices offer puppy parties to help socialize pets.*

A socialization exercise I often use is to take my puppy to a local stately home car park, where there are always crowds of people parking their cars, then disembarking. There is also a play area for children, which gets quite noisy. I raise the tailgate of the car and sit above the bumper, with the puppy safely behind the cage door. I take treats with me, and reward my charge as he shows interest and not fear.

Most veterinary practices run 'puppy parties' now, and this is a good way of socializing, although care needs to be taken regarding the size of other breeds present. If most of the other puppies are of the giant breed, your puppy could be damaged in rough play. Conversely, if the others are of the toy breeds and yours is big by comparison, then it is yours that could do the damaging!

Most areas are served by at least one dog club, and these frequently run socialization classes along with those for obedience and show training. Go and watch on your own to ensure it is what you want before actually taking your puppy.

## Grooming and Bathing

The earlier the puppy becomes used to the brush, comb and shower, the easier it will be. My lot queue up to be groomed, pushing and shoving in their eagerness to be next. Having a dog does *not* mean your house should be covered in hair that moves like tumbleweed every time there is a draught. Nor should it mean that everywhere smells doggy: if your dog and his bedding are clean, then there will not be any unpleasant odours.

### Grooming

Daily grooming will mean that loose hair is deposited in the brush and comb instead of on your floors. Also, you have invested good money and countless hours in your pet, and it is understandable that you should want him to look his best.

#### *Brushing*

The sooner a puppy is accustomed to being groomed, the easier the task will be. I start brushing puppies at eight weeks old, using a very soft brush of the type sold for human babies. Sit the puppy on your lap and gently stroke him with the brush. Start at the back of the neck, brushing the way the coat lies, towards the tail. Pay attention to the tail and the back of the hind legs, because an adult dog is most likely to take exception to these areas being groomed unless he is used to it from an early age. Gently turn the puppy on to his back and brush between his forelegs, his stomach and inside his hind legs.

As he gets older, you can progress to a stiffer brush, but avoid those with wire pins as they are very scratchy, and as this breed is prone to eczema, anything that irritates the

skin should be avoided. If you must use any sort of wire brush, then use a slicker brush for the long feathering of the tail and the backs of the front and hind legs, and underneath the body. Use it extremely lightly as the dog will object (quite rightly) if you apply pressure. Try such a brush on your own hair, and you will be surprised at how very little pressure is applied before it scratches your scalp.

### Combing

Comb the young puppy with a small plastic comb, using it flat against the coat; like this you avoid digging the teeth into the skin. Progress to a steel comb once the puppy reaches four months. Combs with handles are easier to use, and those with wider-spaced teeth are preferable.

There are all sorts of fancy combs available. Some have teeth that pivot and are guaranteed to remove tangles (though if the coat is truly tangled, then only scissors would solve the problem). There are also matt-splitting combs with a blade edge to the teeth – though as long as you spend a few minutes a day grooming your dog, you are never likely to need such a comb.

The humble flea comb is a useful addition to your grooming tools. Not only will it comb out the fleas themselves, but it will also remove their droppings. If you drop the fur and detritus from your comb on to damp kitchen towel, if it stains red you will know your dog has fleas.

### Nails

The nails of baby puppies, as we have seen earlier, need regular trimming to ensure the bitch does not get scratched and become sore. Older puppies that have a hard surface such as concrete or paving to run on, seldom need to have their nails clipped. If you do need to trim

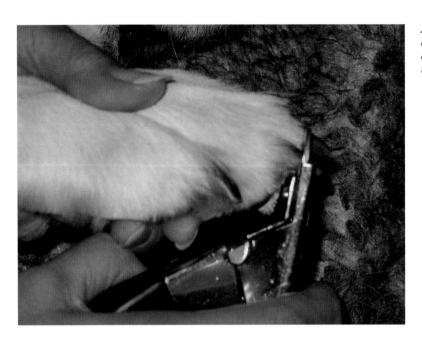

*Allow for the thickness of clippers when estimating how closely to trim the nails.*

back long nails, including dewclaws, ensure it is only the dead end that is removed; the rest of the nail has a 'quick', complete with blood supply, and will bleed profusely and cause the dog pain if your clippers stray into this area.

Nail clippers may be the guillotine type, or the type used for human nails; the former is stronger, but you need to allow for the thickness of the clipper when estimating how closely to trim. The fact that the nail is placed into a notch in the clipper means you are working blind. Other types are not so strong, but better for the inexperienced user.

*Grooming Tables*

Whether you have one dog or several, the grooming table is the most labour-saving device you will own. Bending down to the dog's level is a sure way of having a bad back, and kneeling is even worse. Many tables are sold, but the average handyman can construct one relatively cheaply. Static tables are the cheapest to buy, but the dog still has to be lifted on to these.

Tables that rise to the required level are hydraulic or electric. Hydraulic tables have a foot pedal that you operate to bring the table up to the required level, with the dog on board. The level is raised gradually with each depression of the pedal.

The flagship of the range is the electric table. The dog steps on, and a button starts the table gliding to the level most comfortable for you to work at. As I write I have just bought one of these tables, and cannot imagine why I didn't do it years ago. All those hours of bending and kneeling are now in the past! A useful addition to all these tables is a removable arm to which the dog may be attached, so leaving the owner's hands free. Never leave a dog attached to this unless you are with him, because if he jumped off the table, tragedy could result.

**Bathing**

By far the easiest way to wash the dog is in a shower. A non-slip mat must be used, or the dog's feet will splay and he will panic. It is vitally important to realize that dogs cannot tolerate water of a temperature anywhere approaching that which adult humans can bear. Tepid water, such would be used for bathing a baby, is ideal. Have the shower running with the nozzle of the showerhead on the floor and turned away from the dog before leading him into the shower: like this, you avoid him being frightened by the sudden rush of water as the shower is switched on.

Have the shampoo ready mixed, ideally in a large plastic jug. Ensure the shampoo is designed for bathing dogs at that age, and wear gloves to protect your hands.

One of the most useful shower aids I have ever come across is a large black suction cup with a short length of chain and a clip attached. Applied to a dry shower cubicle wall, this will restrain the dog and can withstand a great deal of pulling.

Wet the dog thoroughly, working from the top of head towards the tail. When he is evenly wet, pour a small quantity of shampoo, working it into a lather. When he is covered in shampoo, start to rinse, again working from neck to tail. Take care around the eyes: I use a face cloth to wash the area. Avoid getting water inside the ears. The same face cloth can be used to gently cleanse the underside of the flap, after the dog gets out of the shower.

*Drying*

Ensure there is a large, non-slip mat on the floor outside the shower. Wrap a large towel over the dog's back and under his belly; this will take the worst of the water as he tries to shake himself. Whether you towel him dry, or use a small hair dryer or one of the professional 'blasters', is a matter of personal choice. I combine the first two of these options.

My dogs love being dried, and are asleep within minutes of the process starting. However, you do need to accustom them to a dryer from the earliest age if they are not to be scared of it.

## Coat Preparations

Grooming aids are big business, but in general, if your dog is fed correctly and in good condition, you should not need to use them. Also you should be aware that, if you are showing your dog, there must not be any preparation in the dog's coat at the time of exhibition or you could be banned. Only a water spray is permitted on show day. Occasionally Goldens will have very dry coats, and if this cannot be corrected by giving evening primrose oil orally, then an oily coat dressing can help. Do not, however, use this during the week before you show your dog in case traces are found. The idea is to condition the coat long before the show.

People have all sorts of weird and wonderful favourite preparations, but only trial and error will enable you to decide which is best for your dog. What suits your friend's dog might not have the desired effect on yours.

I would not recommend the powders sold for 'dry bathing' dogs. I have never found one that works, and the dog leaves powdery deposits where he lies and gives off a cloud of dust every time he moves. The only preparation with which to effectively bath a dog is shampoo and water.

## The Benefits of Grooming and Bathing

Apart from the obvious benefit of making your dog look and feel better, grooming is the best possible bonding exercise. It is extremely therapeutic for the owner, and very good for the dog; it is the time when your pet will have your undivided attention, and in this busy world such moments are rare.

Another benefit is that while you are working on him you have the chance to examine him for undesirable lumps, bumps and sore

*Puppies should be lifted into the car.*

*Puppies derive much exercise from the house and garden.*

*It is essential to lift puppies out of cars, or injury could result.*

patches. You will also be able to check his teeth and inside his ears. Look on each grooming session as a full body inspection.

## Exercise

The bones of puppies are not fully calcified until they are adult, so they must be treated with care; for example, it is not advisable to allow your puppy to race up and down stairs, or even to constantly go up and down steps leading to the garden. Immature joints are relatively softer and react badly to trauma of any kind. It is therefore essential to lift your dog in and out of the car because he could seriously hurt himself jumping in and out himself, and especially jumping out.

### How Much is Enough?

Young puppies derive all the exercise they need by playing in the house and garden. Once vaccinations are over, short walks may become part of your routine, although these are more for socialization purposes than for exercise. It is a sad sight to see a tiny, reluctant puppy being dragged through crowds on a hot day. In summer confine the short walks to each end of the day when it is cooler.

*All dogs love to roll.*

By twelve weeks the puppy can have half an hour's walk on the lead twice a day, with the freedom of the house and garden in between. Do not expect him to accept traffc from the start: cars are noisy and scary, and he needs gradual introduction to them. Ideally sit on the village green and watch the vehicles pass. I sit in the garden of a local stately home, which is always packed with visitors. The car park is at one side, so the puppy hears and sees the vehicles but is generally too busy being petted by visitors to care.

### Increasing the Walks

By five months, an hour of lead walking twice a day would be acceptable. This breed is known to have a predisposition for hip problems, so controlled lead exercise is good for building up the muscles, which would be beneficial to the dog if he were found to have a degree of hip dysplasia later on.

### When a Long Walk is Acceptable

Once your puppy becomes an adult and you have had his hips scored and you know

*Once the adult dog has been found free from hip dysplasia, exercise may become more vigorous.*

he is sound, then the exercise can really increase. If you are planning a good hike, there is no reason why your dog can't accompany you. Be watchful for sheep, as even the best behaved dog cannot resist the

---

### I Want To Be Free!

All dogs need free exercise, but it is becoming increasingly diffcult to find safe areas away from the roads. Should you find such an area, it is impossible to be sure you will not meet another dog of suspect temperament that is also off the lead. A compromise is to use a retractable lead, which allows the dog great freedom, but gives you the control of being able to reel him in, should the need arise.

It is not only other dogs that pose problems for the off-lead dog. Cats, rabbits, and also deer are irresistible to puppies, and any training would be forgotten in the excitement of the moment.

Roads are the greatest threat to dogs running free, and even if you are a considerable distance from a road, it is worth remembering your dog would reach it long before you would.

---

urge to chase. Ensure you have water and a dish for your hike. There are now ingenious bottle-with-dish gadgets with clips so they can attach to a belt or rucksack. Collapsible nylon 'dishes' are available, which are extremely light and portable and, surprisingly, are waterproof.

If you are in sheep country, and particularly if you are walking through heather, examine your dog for ticks on reaching home. These look like warts, and grow rapidly because they feed on your dog's blood. When removing them, be sure you get the whole creature and don't leave the mouthparts attached to the dog, as these would fester.

## To Sum Up

If you train your puppy in a kind and considerate way, and if you feed, groom and exercise him well, you will enjoy up to fifteen years of companionship from a dog you can be proud of. However well he is bred, the way he turns out is up to you: if you get it wrong, a great deal of time will be needed to put it right. And if you get it really wrong, do enlist professional help: a skilled professional behaviourist will be able to show you many ways of resolving any problems. Even the most wayward dog can be trained by those who have the required knowledge. A recent television programme, where celebrities took dogs from shelters and trained them to a competitive level, has illustrated this, and given new hope to many who are battling with diffcult pets.

## Frequently Asked Questions

For a number of years I was the breed correspondent for a weekly canine publication. During this time I received many letters from Golden Retriever owners, requesting advice. Some were from novice owners, but many were from those with more experience. However they originated, all make interesting reading.

**Q.** *My dog came from an animal shelter and had obviously not been groomed regularly. He is aggressive when I attempt to brush and comb him. How can I get him to enjoy these sessions?*
**A.** Most dogs will have an area where they do not object quite as strongly to being groomed. Identify this area, such as the neck, and start by stroking. Have a soft brush ready and make the transition from hand to brush as smooth as possible. Reward at the stroking stage, when the dog permits you to do this, by giving a treat. Try a few gentle brushstrokes, and treat again.

Certain areas, such as the tail and trousers, seem to elicit more objection to grooming than others. Great patience is needed when attempting to groom these places, and you must expect to make haste slowly. Often it will only be possible to groom one or two strands of hair before the dog objects.

If the long hair is very matted, do not attempt to brush and comb, as the pulling on this hair, and the discomfort it causes, will almost certainly meet with an aggressive response. Use a muzzle (one of the kind basket type, which allows the dog to breathe freely and pant, is best), and quickly cut off all the matted hair. Remove the muzzle, praise and treat, and do no more that day.

The very short hair will be knot free and very easy to groom, so just brush two or three times, praise and treat. Follow up with a game or walk.

Persistence will be needed, and it will possibly take more than a month before a dog who is very opposed to grooming will accept it.

**Q.** *I love my dog dearly, but I also love my garden. His digging is turning my previously immaculate lawn into something resembling a rabbit warren. What can I do?*
**A.** Goldens are enthusiastic diggers and are able to dig very large holes in a short time. The only completely satisfactory method of preventing digging is for the dog never to be alone in the garden, or be restricted to a paved area.

Dogs dig for several reasons, including searching for mice, making a 'nest' in preparation for whelping, to bury bones or toys, or to create a cool area in which to lie.

Digging near fences is not only undesirable, but is downright dangerous as it will give the dog a means of escape. All fences should be either sunk into concrete, have slabs at the base, or have a border of coarse shingle which will run back into the hole as the dog digs.

**Q.** *My dog constantly lifts his leg on the same shrubs, which have now turned brown. What can I do to stop him?*
**A.** Once males designate an area for urination, it is almost impossible to stop the habit, unless they are excluded from the spot. Do not replace the dying shrubs with new ones, as your dog will just resume his old habit.

It is possible to buy a post specifically designed for a dog to urinate on, so to replace the ailing shrubs with such a post would be a good idea. In fact, an ordinary wooden post works just as well.

**Q.** *My puppy is delightful in every way except that she insists on biting our hands and feet – and her sharp puppy teeth give quite a bite.*
**A.** It is unlikely that your puppy intends to bite in an aggressive way, but whatever her motives, she needs to be taught that such behaviour is unacceptable.

Usually this biting is in response to the discomfort felt during the teething period, and the need to gnaw on something to relieve the pain.

When the puppy bites your fingers, say 'no' sharply, praising when she stops, and immediately hand her one of the many teething toys that are available in the shops. It should only take a couple of days of such training before she gets the message.

**Q.** *When I bought my puppy, the breeder told me that the adult dogs moult once a year. My dog is now three and seems to moult all the time. Can I do anything to reduce this shedding of hair?*
**A.** This breed has one or two annual moults, but a small quantity of fur is shed throughout the year. If this is excessive, there are several things you can do:

- Different diets may be tried, or it often helps to add evening primrose oil to the present diet (2,000mg per day).
- Spayed bitches and neutered dogs tend to carry profuse, dry coats. As there is a much heavier coat present, when the dog moults there is considerably more shedding than in entire dogs and bitches.
- Bitches that shed excessively often revert to normal coat growth once they have had a litter of puppies. It should be noted that there will be a heavy hair loss from the underside of the bitch immediately prior to whelping.
- Regular, thorough grooming is essential to limit the quantity of hair deposited in the house by moulting dogs. Regular brushing will stimulate new hair growth.

If the dog fails to respond when the above methods are tried, a visit to the vet would be advisable to ascertain whether there is an underlying health problem.

**Q.** *My dog not only eats his own faeces but also cleans up after my other dog. I find the habit repugnant, especially as he enjoys licking my grandchildren.*
**A.** The Golden Retriever is known to have this habit, and in over forty years of keeping the breed, I have never found a cure. When only one dog is kept, it is comparatively easy to remove the opportunity for him to pursue this habit. When two or more are kept it becomes more diffcult, as one simply cannot watch the dogs every moment. Some owners are adamant that adding pineapple to the dog's food prevents the habit, but when I tried this I found that they were keener than ever to clean up the waste.

Tablets are available (sold as 'coprophagia' remedies), but a large number is needed (eight daily, of those I obtained) and they had no effect on my dogs at all.

A friend tried spraying her dog's faeces with disinfectant, and while he appeared to be deterred, he reverted to his former behaviour once the spraying stopped. Besides, it is not really practical to stand with a disinfectant spray waiting for the dog to defecate.

I personally would be *so* relieved if a cure were found, as this habit is the most distasteful part of keeping this lovely breed.

**Q.** *My bitch rolls on dead creatures and other filth we encounter when out walking – she sees it before I do, and is rolling before I catch up with her. I then have to put my smelly dog into my car to drive back home. What can I do to make her realize that this is unacceptable behaviour?*
**A.** This is, I'm afraid, another unsavoury Golden habit, and the only way to stop your dog doing it is to keep her on the lead. Carrying a water pistol and aiming a jet of water as your dog starts to roll will help, as would throwing a lead whilst shouting '*No!*'.

Try to avoid walking where foxes and hedgehogs are common, as it is their droppings that are most favoured by dogs.

**Q.** *My dog has a bout of diarrhoea about once a week, although I never change his food. Why does he do this?*
**A.** It is possible that your dog is chewing something which upsets him. Goldens are addicted to wood in any form, and will chew sections of fencing, given the chance, and regularly chew sticks which they find on walks.

If you have children, ensure that the dog is not being given unsuitable titbits. Sometimes these 'treats' are given to disguise the fact their family members do not want to eat their own meals.

If the problem persists, take a faeces sample to the vet for examination. Most infrequent bouts of diarrhoea are harmless, but some are an indication of more serious problems.

**Q.** *My Golden has been rubbing his rear end along the carpet and is frequently licking under his tail. He is wormed regularly, so that is not the cause.*
**A.** The cause is almost certainly a problem with his anal glands. These emit a minute quantity of foul-smelling liquid which served as a marker when dogs were evolving.

These glands now provide no useful function; they sometimes become full and then cause great irritation to the dog, which attempts to gain relief by scooting along the carpet. It is possible to ascertain if these glands are full by grasping the root of the tail and raising it. This will cause several drops of fluid to be released, and the smell will leave you in no doubt as to its origin. Ensure you do this outside, as such drops on the carpet would be diffcult to clean.

Sometimes it is possible to improve the problem by feeding a bulkier diet, but it has been my experience that dogs who suffer from anal gland problems do so throughout their lives.

The only treatment is to have the vet empty these glands on a regular basis (before an abscess results). If they are very infected, an antibiotic will be given at the time of emptying. In extreme cases, the glands must be removed; however, it is a deep incision and healing is slow.

**Q.** *My dog will need medication in tablet form for the rest of her life. However hard I try, even when she appears to have swallowed the tablet, she spits it out later. I dread this daily battle and would like to know what other methods I could try.*
**A.** Dogs are very adept at concealing tablets but, luckily, they are not very bright, and tend not to notice if you hide them in food. Soft treats with a hole in the middle are now sold for the purpose of administering pills. I give one without a pill first, then conceal the pill in the second one.

Other ideas are to cut cubes of corned beef and hide the pill there. Cocktail sausages are a perfect size for hiding tablets. Bread, thickly spread with butter and folded over the tablet, works well. New potatoes conceal tablets adequately.

Dogs that are suspicious when you hand them food in which tablets are concealed, will usually respond well if you roll the food along the floor, so making it into a game.

Although this does not apply for your dog's present medication, if you need to administer liquid, do not even consider using a spoon, as most will be spilled. Dose your dog by using a syringe (without a needle): the plastic nozzle will fit into the side of the lips and between the teeth. Depress the plunger slowly, as a swift squirt would make the dog jerk his head away, so spilling some of the liquid.

**Q.** *We expected our Golden to chew when he was a puppy but at two years old the habit is as bad as ever. His favourite objects are chair and table legs, which now resemble sharpened pencils. We refuse to use a cage, believing them to be cruel, but we really love our home, which is being destroyed at an alarming rate.*
**A.** Your dog can only pursue his trail of destruction when you are not around to stop him, so you need to limit the length of time he is on his own.

Generally dogs only chew if they are bored, but there are some who do it for sheer enjoyment! The more tired your dog is, the less inclined he will be to chew; it is sometimes simply a matter of breaking the habit. A good programme of hard exercise, followed by play, will distract him from chewing; such play should involve 'mind game' play such as the cubes and balls in which treats may be concealed. These fall out at random as the dog noses the toy around the floor.

Such activity will keep him occupied for a while, and when he finishes playing, he should settle down to sleep rather than to chew. And take care never to use food-based toys with more than one dog at once, or disagreements could occur.

**Q.** *I have always wanted to have a Golden Retriever and a kitten at the same time, and now that I have retired from work, I am in a position to do this. However, I am not sure how to introduce a puppy and a kitten to each other.*
**A.** The good thing about introducing baby animals to each other is that they seem quite unaware that they are from a different species. The kitten will need a bolt hole for when play becomes too rough, but will have the advantage of being able to jump up to a higher level, out of the puppy's way.

If the puppy is too rough for the kitten at the start, introduce them with the kitten in a cage; this way, each can become familiar with the other, without accidents happening.

When dogs and cats are introduced at an early age, there is seldom a problem. The cat will almost always be in charge, and even tiny kittens are surprisingly feisty!

One word of warning: if your kitten has a litter tray it will need to be kept well out of the puppy's way or he will clean up the contents!

Never leave the two unattended until you are positive that they will come to no harm. This will generally be several months after the initial introduction.

**Q.** *My last dog was travel sick all her life. How can I avoid the same thing happening with my new puppy?*
**A.** Ideally, puppies should have car rides when they are under eight weeks old. Frequently, it is not practical to take puppies on a car journey until after they are old enough to go to their new homes. By then, the fear factor has become established and careful handling is needed to retrain the puppy to like travelling and not be upset by it.

Puppies are less likely to be sick if someone is holding them. If left alone in the car, even in a cage, they tend to be thrown about and the movement will make them vomit.

Years ago, any medication given by vets would make dogs very sleepy, but better drugs are available now, which do not make the eyelids droop, nor will the dog sleep for hours. Take care not to feed a puppy before a car journey or he will be sick. A car harness will stop him being thrown about, in the absence of someone to hold him.

**Q.** *How do I stop my adult Golden from jumping up? He does it with visitors and with us.*
**A.** It is easy to cure this habit but all those involved need to be consistent in the way they react. If he does it when you are standing up, ignore him, turning your back on him as you do so. This will cause him to slide down, and as soon as he does, praise him.

When you are seated and he jumps up, stand up instantly, making a loud 'Ah Ah' noise. Praise instantly when he gets down. Although it is quite exhausting to keep jumping to your feet, this method works really quickly and is worth persisting with.

**Q.** *My much loved Golden died recently aged thirteen years. The whole family is heart-broken, and although I would eventually like another dog, I feel it is disloyal to replace her.*
**A.** The pain of losing a dog which has been an important part of the family is just as real and diffcult to bear as the death of a human family member. It is sometimes helpful to give yourself time to grieve before thinking of acquiring another dog. If you do so too soon, there might be a tendency to compare the new dog with the one you have just lost.

It is important to accept that you will not be replacing the pet you have lost but will be getting another that, in time, will help to heal the hurt you are feeling just now.

# 4  Showing Your Dog

*Showing dogs is addictive.*

Many people start to show as a result of others admiring their dog and saying 'He's really lovely. Why don't you show him?' It is a hobby that, once started, may soon develop into an obsession.

## Types of Show

There are various levels of showing, namely charity shows, limited shows, open, breed club and championship shows.

### Charity Shows
Some derive pleasure from attending charity shows where classes are available for both pedigree and non-pedigree dogs. The classification is broad and the pedigree classes will cater for many breeds, shown against each other. There will also be novelty classes such

as 'The Dog with the Waggiest Tail', or 'The Dog Most Like its Owner'. Entry fees are low and the prizes are generally rosettes.

### Limited Shows
The next type of show is the 'limited' one. To exhibit at these shows you must be a member of the organizing society, but membership is very cheap, and again, so are entry fees. Classes are for pedigree dogs that are registered with the Kennel Club in the ownership of the person entering the dog, and most classes are open to several breeds. The terrier class could include all dogs classified as such by the Kennel Club. Many societies will highlight a different breed each year by having classes for that specific breed. Awards at such shows are usually rosettes and dog-related prizes in kind.

### Open Shows
At open shows many breeds are classified, which means that breeds will only be shown against others of their own breed; thus Golden Retrievers would meet other Golden Retrievers and be judged with them. The dogs are each judged by being compared with the Kennel Club's breed standard, which is a blueprint for what the breed should look like, and how it should move.

There could be as few as four classes for each breed at an open show, or as many as ten, and the classification will start with the 'Puppy' class, which is for dogs and bitches of six months to one year old. The highest class is the 'Open', which is for all eligible dogs of

*The author showing a young bitch at a breed club's open show.*

## Breed Club Shows

These may be open or championship shows, but are confined to a single breed, with entries being fractionally cheaper for those who are members of the clubs. Classes are separate for dogs and bitches, and there is usually one judge for each sex. Whether the shows are held at championship or open level, the best dog and best bitch compete at the end of judging for 'Best in Show'. The best dog and best bitch puppy will compete for 'Best Puppy in Show'.

## Championship Shows

The championship show is the highest level of show, and it is also the most expensive, with each class costing in excess of £20 to enter. Most do not give prize money and, as at the other shows, rosettes and cards constitute the awards.

the breed. This is not an age class, as the Puppy class, so it is possible for a very young dog to be entered alongside a six year-old.

Entry fees at open shows are low, but there is often no prize money, or just £1 for first prize. Generally the awards are prize cards and rosettes.

It is at such shows that champions are made. The best of each sex wins a challenge certificate, and three of these certificates, awarded by three different judges, are required for a dog to take the title of 'Show Champion'. To be a full champion, a Golden

*The final line-up.*

*Judging in progress at a championship show.*

Retriever also requires a 'Show Gundog Working Certificate' to prove he is proficient in the basics of the work he was bred to do.

The dog and bitch that win the challenge certificates compete against each other for the coveted 'Best of Breed' award. Dogs winning this then go forward to compete in the Gundog Group. Eventually the winners of all the groups compete for 'Best in Show' – and there can be few who have not witnessed the hype surrounding this final at Crufts. The huge European shows make even more of this, with laser light shows and equestrian displays.

## Entering a Show

The entries for shows close well in advance of the event (apart from charity shows, where entries are taken on the day). Notice of these shows is given in the two-weekly canine newspapers, and there are now several sites on the internet that give information about forthcoming shows: typing 'dog shows' into your search engine should give the required information. Championship show entries close a month or more before the show.

To enter a show you will require a schedule that includes an entry form. The method of entry is self-explanatory, and requires details of your dog's parentage and its age. There is a space for the number of classes you wish to enter. Most societies now have facilities for entering online, and as a receipt can be printed immediately, this is a safer way than sending an entry by post, and not knowing whether or not it has been received.

If you enter an open show, you will receive nothing through the post. The exception to this is if the open show is being held in conjunction with an agricultural show, when you will receive a car park pass and admission passes for you and your dog. Championship show societies send out passes for dogs, handlers and cars.

## Getting Started

It is important that you train your dog to show before you even think of entering, or you will waste your money. Ringcraft classes are held in most areas, and the Kennel Club will give details where your nearest is

*The author's promising five month-old puppy.*

*The same bitch, now two years old, who has fulfilled her early promise.*

situated. It is a good idea to go along to the training session without your dog on the first occasion, as this will give you a chance to see what is expected of it, and will give you time to assimilate what you have seen before embarking on the training proper.

At ringcraft classes, owners are taught to get the very best from their dogs; amongst other things the dogs will learn how to stand and have their teeth and bodies examined without showing apprehension. (Accustoming them to such examinations also makes visits to the vet

*Dogs derive much pleasure from being shown.*

*It is essential for puppies of all breeds to socialize.*

much easier!) The aim in these classes is to replicate the activity and atmosphere of a show as closely as possible. Trainers will be 'judges', and dogs will learn to stand in a show pose and also to move in a controlled manner, which shows off their good points.

Group socialization is practised, because even if your dog is the best specimen of his breed, it will not benefit him at all if he cannot interact well with other dogs and people. He will learn to accept other dogs and to regard them as friends. Everything that happens at these classes should be geared towards making him confident with humans and other dogs – and the most important point to make regarding these sessions is that they should be enjoyable.

Do not automatically join the first class that you observe. If the general ambience is not to your liking, then find one that is. It is

*Regular training is needed for dogs to perform well at shows.*

63

important that you feel at ease with your surroundings, because if you are not relaxed, then you cannot expect your dog to be. Dogs are extremely intuitive when it comes to their owner's feelings.

**Practice At Home**
As well as attending weekly show-training classes you will need to continue the lessons at home, and to do this effectively, you will have to enlist the help of people your dog is not familiar with. Family members are all very well, but they will not help accustom the dog to being handled by strangers.

Encourage your dog to submit to an examination of his teeth. This is not like a human dental inspection, where the patient is required to present a wide-open mouth: judges simply need to assess the 'bite', which is how well the teeth fit together in the required scissor formation. The dog's mouth is therefore left closed, and the judge will just lift the lips to assess the desired alignment.

The dog must allow the angle of his neck and shoulder to be examined, and his front legs felt and his feet lifted for inspection. Judges will feel the ribs to see if they are of the desired shape and length, and to assess if the dog has the required short couplings, which is where the ribcage ends and the hind leg begins.

The bend of the dog's stifle and hocks will need to be examined, and the position of the tail will also be assessed: it should be set neither high nor low, but level with the back.

To check for the correct double coat – a harsher outer coat with softer, fluffer fur underneath – the judge will run a hand against the way the coat lies naturally.

Of all the areas to be examined, the dog is most likely to be nervous about the judge handling his head and tail, so you will probably have to spend the most time accustoming him to these parts being handled. It helps if you pat and stroke your dog in these areas

from puppyhood. Generally it is the bitches that most dislike having their tails examined, and the best way to get over this is to handle your puppy's tail from the beginning, as soon as you take it home. If, however, you only decide to show your bitch once she is adult, then patience is needed.

You should ensure that you only ever touch and handle the tail gently and in a way that the dog will find pleasurable. Talk to her, and at the same time stroke and lift the tail gently, without making too much fuss about it, or she will get the idea that something scary is about to happen and will react nervously. Once she is accustomed to you and your family stroking, brushing and lifting her tail, enlist the help of people she doesn't know to repeat these exercises.

If you have stroked your dog's head from the time he was a baby, you are halfway towards him accepting having his head examined. Judges will cup their hands on each side of the head to assess the shape; at the same time they will look for the required dark (but never black) eye colour, and will check that the head is balanced – the muzzle should be of equal length with the forehead. Also there should not be creases, giving a frowning effect, nor 'calf licks', where a ridge of fur runs in the opposite direction from the rest of the coat; these ridges are most frequently found between the eyes or across the muzzle.

**Patience is Needed**
Training for showing, in common with all other forms of training, cannot be accomplished in a few days. Little and often is the secret, and it is vitally important that all lessons are short and enjoyable. Keep the sessions lighthearted, or your dog will become bored and will dread the next lesson. I would never train my dog for more then ten minutes twice a day. Follow the session with something the dog really enjoys, such as playing with a favourite toy.

*Shows are enjoyable
social occasions.*

Vary where you train your dog, because if he is to be shown he will need to perform in a variety of locations; parks, friends' gardens and car parks make good training grounds. Remember that the dog that behaves well when moving on concrete will often be a perfect fool on grass. Moreover, many shows are held in fields where farm animals have been grazing, and Goldens are notorious for either rolling in, or eating their droppings, so be prepared for such antics!

*Trimming to perfection
takes many years.*

65

# Trimming

Your Golden cannot attend shows in his natural growth of coat, which is too long and untidy. Trimming to perfection takes many years, but once you have been shown how to do it, you will make a passable job in your first year. The secret of good trimming is that when you have completed the task it should be impossible to see where the scissors have been, and the dog should look perfectly natural. While no amount of brilliant trimming can ever compensate for a poorly constructed dog, a professional trim will make a mediocre dog look better, and a very good dog superb. One reason that judges actually handle dogs is to ensure that a really clever trimmer has not disguised serious faults.

## Equipment
*Scissors*
You will never trim a dog well with cheap scissors of poor quality, so invest in the best you can afford, and never use them for anything else. At a recent show I absent-mindedly snipped off a nettle touching my arm, and that lapse of concentration meant my scissors had to go for sharpening because the woody stem caused a minute notch in the blades.

Good quality scissors will last indefinitely, but you only realize how blunt they have become once you use them for the first time after sharpening. If you intend showing and therefore trimming several dogs, it is worth having two sets of everything, so that one is always razor sharp.

At the very least you will need thinning scissors and a pair with a straight edge. Thinners are of two types: those with a toothed blade and a straight-edged one; and those with both blades toothed. The former takes off more fur at each snip, so is not the best type for the novice trimmer. Try those with both blades toothed when you begin, because when you make a few cuts in error, it will not be so obvious.

Short, straight-edged scissors make short cuts, so use the longest blade that you feel confident with. When trimming the tail it would be impossible to attain the required straight edge with short blades.

*The basic equipment for trimming.*

Curved scissors are an extremely useful asset, and now that I use them regularly, I cannot imagine why it took me so long to acquire a pair. Feet and ears have curved edges, so it makes sense to trim them with curved blades.

If you only trim a single dog on a regular basis you will need to have your scissors sharpened at least once a year, but ideally twice. Many manufacturers offer a postal sharpening service that is fast and effective, and several championship shows have stallholders offering an on-site sharpening service.

*Nail Clippers*

Nail clippers are an essential part of the grooming kit, although even experienced owners feel moments of unease when clipping nails because each nail has a sensitive 'quick' in the centre, which will bleed profusely if nicked. It is safer to err on the side of caution, clipping wide of this area, which is pinker (except in nails that are wholly black). If you feel too worried about cutting nails, vets and grooming parlours offer the service.

It is a complete fallacy that dogs exercised on concrete have short nails, whereas those running on grass have long nails; in fact breeding decides which dogs have short or long nails. If your Golden has long nails you will need to trim them throughout his life, besides which as dogs get older, the nails show more growth and will need clipping more frequently. Always pay special attention to the dew claws, because these grow faster than the others and will grow full circle, back into the flesh if left unattended.

Clippers come in various designs. The guillotine type is my choice, but many people prefer those resembling secateurs. Filing is another way of keeping nails short, either by hand or with the newer, battery-operated file. Many dogs are rather put off by the noise of the latter.

**The Task of Trimming**

I start with the ears, trimming around the edges with the curved blades. Do not push into the fur, but just take off the tips of the hairs, rounding the point of the ear. Avoid accidentally cutting the double fold of skin at the base of the ear.

*The edge of the ear is trimmed with curved scissors.*

I then trim the flap with thinning scissors, making upward cuts in the natural direction of the fur. I am frequently asked, when I give demonstrations, how I know when I've

*The hair on top of the ear flap needs to be thinned.*

*Where the ear joins the cheek, there is thick fur, which needs to be thinned.*

*Using thinning scissors, the chest hair is trimmed in an upward direction.*

taken enough off. Be ever mindful of the fact that if you take off too much, it will take several months to grow back. I want the ear flap to have fur almost as short as a Labrador's ear.

After the ears comes the most diffcult part of the dog to trim, the 'shirt front' or chest hair. This is an area where your wrong cuts will be painfully obvious, so be prepared to make haste slowly. I suggest that you comb after each two snips, because this way you can monitor the effect at every stage. You need to poke the thinners into the fur in an upward direction. Great care is needed if you have a mid- to dark-coloured Golden, because unless you are conscious of only taking out the undercoat, you will expose large patches of the paler fur beneath and your dog will have a patchwork-quilt effect. This takes months to grow back and would keep your dog out of the show ring for a long time.

For the trimming on the front of the dog, you need to cut very closely at throat level and gradually come out to the point of the breastbone. It must look natural, and anything approaching the final effect of a poodle trim is undesirable.

To trim the feet, place the dog so he is lying on his side. Pull up the long hair between his toes and trim this off with the thinning scissors. Neaten around the edge of the feet, where the toes meet the pads, using your curved scissors. Nail trimming follows naturally at this point, and you will need to neaten up the edges, around the pad margins, as the nails are shortened.

*Hair between the toes is tidied.*

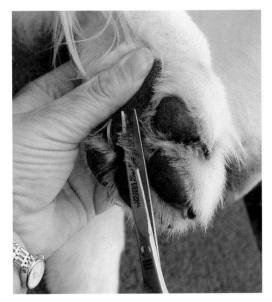

*Tidy hair between the pads, but do not wholly remove it.*

Thick tufts of hair grow between the pads under the feet. This is the buffer between the surfaces – many of them uneven – that your dog will walk on, and his sensitive pads, so it would be quite wrong to remove this fur altogether; however, is a good idea to neaten it.

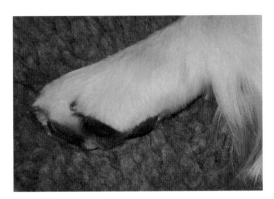

*This foot is almost completed.*

While your dog is still on his side, brush the feathering at right angles to the leg. Using thinners, trim the long hair at the back of the pastern to give a clean appearance. With straight-edged scissors, trim the tip of the feathering, which should resemble the shape of a cook's knife when finished.

Brush the feathering under the body straight down, and with straight scissors, trim off any straggly ends. Males grow profuse feathering, and if this is left long and straggly, can make the dog appear short on the leg. This is no more than an optical illusion, but one that could spoil your dog's chances when shown under an inexperienced judge.

*Leg feathering is neatened by trimming the tips.*

The back feet need to be trimmed in the same way as the front ones. Brush the fluffy hair on the hock in an upward direction,

*Excess hair on the hock is revealed.*

*Thinning scissors are used to neaten hock hair.*

and trim off half the length with thinning scissors.

While the dog is still lying down, brush the feathering on the tail so it resembles a thick fringe at right angles from the tail bone. Hold the bony tip of the tail between finger and thumb, and trim towards the root using straight-edged scissors. Again, the desired shape, when finished, is that of a cook's knife.

*The tail is brushed out in a fan shape.*

Goldens grow very thick tails, and you will need to have the dog in a standing position to see how the work is progressing. Shake the tail, and stray hairs will come down and show that your line is nowhere near as straight as you thought.

Place the dog in a lying position, on the opposite side from where you first started the tail. Brush out and trim until you reach the desired effect. The dog needs to stand again and you can trim straggly hairs from

the 'trousers' which hang over the hock. Left untrimmed, this looks particularly untidy when the dog moves away from the judge.

*Start trimming with straight-edged scissors, shaking the tail to reveal straggly ends.*

*Trim the tail from both sides.*

## Little and Often

To trim successfully, so it is not too much of a chore for you and your dog, it is a good idea to start mid-week for a weekend show. I can trim a fully coated dog to show condition in an hour, but I've had years of practice. You will be very slow to start with, but do not despair because you will speed up as your confidence grows.

## Bathing for Shows

Some like to bath before trimming but I prefer to do it afterwards. Bathing softens the coat,

*Regular grooming and trimming results in an immaculately presented dog.*

*Stand clear when bathing a dog outside!*

and soft hair is harder to trim. Many exhibitors prefer to bath their dogs several days before the show to enable the natural oils to return to the coat. With a blonde dog it doesn't always work to bath early as the dog may become grubby before the day. I know one successful exhibitor who maintained she had never bathed her dog!

Mine certainly look much better after a bath. I bathed five of them for a photo shoot this week and felt so proud of their squeaky clean appearance! Of course, they couldn't wait to have a good roll as soon as their moment of fame was over!

## Show Day

### The Show Bag
You will need a show bag, which you can pack the night before or on the day of the show. The bag itself needs to be lightweight and waterproof, and have either a shoulder strap or two straps so it may be carried as a back-pack; with a dog in one hand and folding chair in the other, you will have plenty to cope with. The bag will be your means of survival for the duration of the show. Most shows offer catering facilities, and the schedule usually states whether refreshments are on offer, but even so, it is convenient to take part of your needs for the day. Queuing is not easy with a dog, neither is carrying a hot drink.

Our climate being notoriously unpredictable, you must take the means of cleaning and drying your dog, should it become necessary. There are absorbent cloths that soak up many times their own weight in water, and these are very useful for taking most of the water out of the dog's coat. A towel is essential: remember to leave more dry towels in your car for emergencies.

You will need a brush and comb. The comb should be small enough to fit in your pocket for last-minute grooming in the ring; the brush ideally should be pure bristle.

If you use titbits to bait your dog in the ring, ensure your pocket is large enough to accommodate them. Handy waist bags are available, and save pockets becoming greasy. These bags have compartments for car keys and money, which would not be safe to leave at the ringside.

Your dog will need water, and a good tip is to place a bottle of water in the freezer the night before the show; it will slowly thaw en route to the show, so giving your dog a colder drink than water taken from the tap. Remember the water dish.

If you are travelling overnight to a distant show, ensure you pack a meal to give your dog after judging is completed. The dry foods are preferable to canned meals, as they are clean and leave no smell afterwards.

The show lead must be packed, and I always keep this in a waterproof pouch in case anything leaks and stains the lead on the way to the show.

If the show is a championship one, your dog will be required to be on a bench, so a thick, slip-proof rug will be needed. A bench chain will secure your dog on to the bench. Open shows are more relaxed occasions, where handlers and dogs sit round the ring; for this you will need a chair, and your dog will need a rug to keep him clean – even on a summer morning the grass will be damp, so a waterproof-backed rug is preferable. A pin is required to secure your ring number, although some people prefer the plastic holder, which has an elastic tie to fit round your arm.

Something my bag is never without is a bottle of fluid for cleaning dirty marks from dogs' coats. Many times my dogs brush against the exhaust pipe as they get out of the car, so acquiring a sooty deposit on their pristine fur. This cleaner is spirit-based, dries quickly and leaves no stain.

Coat sprays are another issue: many are sold but all are frowned upon by our Kennel Club unless no residue is left in the coat. Spot checks are done on coats at shows, and any found to have unnatural deposits would result in disciplinary action. You will see many exhibitors spraying their dogs with oils,

glosses and finishing sprays, but be warned that the only safe spray is clear water!

## What to Wear

It is the dog who is on show, not the handler, but this does not mean that dress is unimportant. The handler forms a backdrop to the dog, and has the opportunity to enhance the effect. Only a foolish handler would wear cream trousers when handling a light-coloured dog; conversely, tan trousers would render indistinct the outline of a rich golden dog. The handler's clothing should be neat and unfussy. The full skirt that looks attractive outside the ring will wrap round the dog, obscuring him from the judge's view when moving in the ring. Shoes should enable the free movement of the handler.

It is amusing to see the change that takes place in the wardrobe of the dog owner. Most forsake their dark designer suits for garments that have cavernous pockets for bait and are of colours that do not show paw prints and dog hair!

## On Arrival

Arrive early so that your day begins calmly. Find your ring, and place your chair and dog's rug in a position where you can see the judging and where your dog will be in the shade. Ensure your dog has had a walk and a chance to relieve himself. You will need to collect your catalogue from the secretary's table; this will enable you to see which dogs are entered in your class, and will tell you your ring number. This number will be handed to you as you enter the ring at the beginning of your class (or will be placed on your bench at some championship shows).

In this country, we may stand in any order in the class, whereas in the rest of Europe, dogs stand in numerical order. This gives handlers in the UK an advantage, as no one wants to stand between two top-sized dogs if their own is a little small; neither do we want to stand between profusely coated dogs if ours has recently moulted! As a newcomer, you would be advised to stand last in the ring, as this will give your dog a chance

*It is thrilling to be placed at your first show.*

to settle, and will allow you to see what is going on.

Once all entrants are assembled, the judge will walk round for an initial look at the dogs, then you will be asked to move round the ring together, once or twice. Then each dog will be judged individually by moving to the middle of the ring. This is where your training will be tested as the judge examines your dog. They will then ask you to move him, and this is generally done in a triangular pattern. With the dog on your left side, you will move to the right-hand corner, across the top of the ring to the left-hand corner, and diagonally back to the judge. Sometimes you will then be requested to go 'up and down' or 'to the corner', which is self-explanatory.

When each dog has been seen, all will return to stand around the ring. The judge will walk past each dog, occasionally requesting one to move again. Then the winning line-up will be chosen. In the UK we place dogs from first to fourth (or even down to seventh place at the very large shows); in the rest of Europe, exhibits are placed in reverse order, so if you are pulled out last, you have won!

Much has been resting on your debut into the world of showing and, understandably, you will be disappointed if you are unplaced. Try to be pleased if your dog has remembered some of his training and has enjoyed his day out. Remember to applaud the winner, because on another day it will be your dog in first place, and it is upsetting if the applause is thin. Most importantly, accept that even if you were unplaced, you are still taking the best dog home.

Remember to praise your dog, then give him a drink and a chance to relieve himself before you embark on the journey home.

It is helpful to keep a show diary, in which you can record notes to help your future performance. Whilst it is fresh in your mind, write down how your dog performed, and how you could both improve.

Should you be placed on your first outing, you will wait with great impatience for the weekly dog papers to appear, because there you will see your dog's name in print as a winner. If you have been first at an open show, you will receive a written critique from the judge. At championship shows both the first- and second-placed dogs in each class receive a critique.

As your dog settles down for a well-earned sleep on reaching home after his very first show, are you preparing for an early night? Of course not! You are busy filling in entry forms for your next shows!

# 5 Feeding the Adult

Long gone are the days when the family pet was fed with scraps left over from the table. Dog owners progressed from this most unsatisfactory method of feeding, to one that sadly was not a great deal better: this involved the collection of meat from the local abattoir, much of it classed as unfit for human consumption, and most dogs were fed this meat raw, mixed with bread. In the light of the knowledge we have now of the dangers of feeding raw, condemned flesh, it is surprising that so many dogs remained healthy.

It is interesting to note that hounds in Hunt kennels are still fed raw flesh, usually fallen stock from farms, or road kill. In defence of feeding such food it should be observed that few dogs are healthier or in better condition than hounds.

As regards biscuits, large, hard ones initially became available for dog feeding, though it was customary to feed these with the abattoir meat. These hard biscuits were closely followed by smaller round or oval shapes, which first appeared as plain or charcoal varieties, and eventually became available in mixed colours and flavours.

Eventually biscuit meal appeared, which was intended to be fed with the new tinned foods that became available at around the same time. There was very little choice of either dry or tinned foods, and it was a case of using what was on offer. In London, in the 1940s, the Cats' Meat Man was a common sight, and pet owners would provide their own containers, into which a slithering mass of lungs and intestines was poured. One can only speculate at the level of bacteria present, as this offal was trundled round the streets, on hot days closely pursued by a cloud of flies! Nevertheless the dogs and cats seemed to fare well on this dubious diet.

No self-respecting London dog would be without his bone, usually a large, uncooked shin bone, and it was a common sight to see dogs emerging from the butchers' shops, carrying their own bones home.

In the seventies there was a revolution in dog feeding, when the first complete diets became available. We, as dog owners and breeders, were highly suspicious of this new-fangled food, and rumours abounded as to what these diets contained. Our suspicions were to be proved ill-founded, and today more dogs eat complete diets than any other type of food.

## Complete Diets

As the name suggests, these foods constitute a complete canine nutrition. No additives are needed, and for breeders this has been a welcome advance, because in the early days we did a great deal of harm by supplementing our dog's food with various vitamins and oils. (The harm caused is covered in Chapter 8.)

Apart from the obvious benefit of all ingredients being present in correct proportions, the other advantage for the dog owner is the ease with which such food may be fed: it is literally a case of tipping the required quantity into a dish and offering it to the dog. It is clean, it smells pleasant, and dogs really like it.

*Fresh water must be freely available.*

## What is a Balanced Diet?

A 'balanced' diet consists of fats, proteins, minerals, carbohydrates, vitamins and water; water is needed in larger quantities than the other nutrients. Fats are an essential part of the body's ability to maintain a healthy immune system; they are also needed for healthy skin and a good, glossy coat.

Protein has been discussed at greater length by vets and dog breeders than the rest of the nutrients. It has been suggested that the feeding of excess protein is a contributing factor to osteochondrosis, and that continued feeding of excessive quantities leads to kidney damage. Many adult dogs are fed quantities of protein that are in excess of what the body is able to use, and it is suggested that only pregnant and lactating bitches need protein in excess of 20 per cent. Foods containing 18 per cent protein are perfectly adequate for a maintenance diet, as much above this is merely excreted.

Fibre in the diet binds water in the large intestine so that firmer stools are produced. It also makes the dog feel full. Feeding too much fibre produces flatulence and a large quantity of faeces, both of which make dog-owning difficult. Vitamins and minerals are needed in minute quantities to keep the dog healthy; indeed, the adult dog will derive all the minerals he requires from a balanced diet. The complete foods have very carefully measured quantities, and the urge to supplement the dog's vitamin and mineral intake should be resisted, unless this is specifically instructed by a vet. Over-supplementation may lead to orthopaedic problems, which were much more prevalent in the early years, when we all guessed at quantities.

### What Else is Available?

However vast the range of complete diets, there will always be some dogs that simply do not like being fed in this way, and an alternative is to feed a good quality canned dog food

I have always fed such food to my dogs with the addition of a small quantity of water: it isn't necessary to soak the food, merely to pour on water immediately before feeding. I use one cup of water for each bowl of food. There are dogs who loathe the addition of water to their food, so then food must be given dry, but water should be nearby, fresh and in uninterrupted supply. This is the case whether food is given moistened or dry, but is even more essential for dogs that are eating a dry meal.

The advantage of adding a quantity of water to the dog's food is that it tends to stop its desire to drink vast quantities of water immediately after eating. This causes the meal to swell far more rapidly than would result from the natural gastric juices acting upon it, and will sometimes cause the dog to vomit, or bloat may result.

The varieties of foods available in this range are vast, and there will definitely be a flavour to suit the most finicky eater (although Goldens do not often have this problem!).

with a mixer meal. Again, many flavours are available as canned diets, and dogs seem to enjoy such food. Even so, however much dogs enjoy canned food, a number of Goldens simply cannot tolerate it, and diarrhoea will result. Sometimes dogs that are upset by canned foods fed with a mixer meal can tolerate the canned food perfectly well if it is mixed with rice or pasta.

### Fussy Feeders

Little causes the owner to despair as much as having a dog that is a poor eater, because such dogs remain disinterested no matter what selection of the very best foods is offered to them. The pet dog that is a fussy feeder is easier to deal with than the show dog, brood bitch or stud dog, which must be kept in top condition.

Bitches that are normally good eaters will frequently develop bizarre eating habits when pregnant. I had one that simply refused all dog food, but as she was heavily pregnant, it was vitally important that she ate something. She completed her pregnancy and produced ten healthy puppies after being fed custard creams and pork sausages! I do not advocate such diets, but in this bitch's case it was better that she had some food, however odd her preference. The day after her puppies were born, she reverted to her formerly normal eating habits.

Dogs that are fussy eaters will often eat dog food if it is offered with a small quantity of grated cheese added. For very fussy eaters, it sometimes encourages them to eat if the cheese is melted on the food. Another tip is that the addition of pilchards or sardines makes food irresistible to dogs. Furthermore, most dogs adore pasta, and the addition of this to their regular food will normally encourage them to eat.

Yorkshire puddings and roast potatoes are a useful addition to the food of dogs lacking in bodyweight. Show devotees are familiar with feeding this way. My young champion male enjoys a thick sandwich of bread and corned beef in addition to his dog food; it is diffcult to keep weight on him, and this helps. He also has raw lamb mince.

## Specific Diets

### Invalid and Convalescent Feeding

For both sick and recovering dogs it is vital to keep the diet light and nutritious, and my staple food for such dogs is white fish and boiled rice. Obviously this could not be fed indefinitely as it lacks nutrients, but for a limited period it is unbeatable. Boiled chicken and rice is also a good meal for a sick or recovering dog – though be aware that some Goldens do not tolerate chicken. It is strange, because they cope with turkey perfectly well, but there is something about chicken which upsets them.

### Prescription Diets

Many special diets are available from veterinary surgeries. There are foods for dogs with sensitive digestions, and for those who need a fat-free diet. There are also diets for those suffering from kidney problems and for those unable to tolerate various ingredients commonly found in non-prescription dog foods.

Gluten-free foods are available as prescription diets, but can now be freely obtained, as many of the dog food manufacturers produce them. In fact, there are prescription diets for virtually every known canine condition. They are not cheap, but for some there are no alternatives, and the dog simply would not survive unless fed this way.

### Vegetarian Diets

There are several vegetarian diets available, though I am not sure why one would feed a dog, which is a carnivore, on a meat-free food, unless the reason is ethical – and I do feel it is a little unfair to inflict one's beliefs on the dog. However, I do know of several dogs that are fed in this way, and they appear remarkably healthy.

---

### Faeces

For the town dweller who keeps several dogs, the quantity of waste they produce is important. There is no doubt that some foods produce more waste than others, but it is a trial and error situation, as a food that causes one dog to produce large quantities of faecal matter, will not necessarily result in the same amount of waste when fed to other dogs. If your dog is producing what you consider to be too much waste – though remember, Goldens are large dogs, so do produce quite a lot – experiment with other foods until you find one on which he thrives but produces less waste.

I am frequently asked how many times a day a dog should empty his bowels, and I am not sure there is an average figure. All dogs should go at least once a day, and most will relieve themselves twice. I would say that if your dog habitually empties more than three times a day, he should have a veterinary check to see if he has an absorption problem or a food intolerance. If he tests positive for either condition, it might be resolved by a simple change of food, or a prescription diet might be needed.

---

## Other Foods

### Milk

I have long held the opinion that milk from cows is neither a natural, nor a desirable food for the adult dog. Nor do I believe that puppies need it once they are no longer feeding from their mothers. The exception to this is goats' milk, which is easily digested and attractive to dogs.

Goldens do not tolerate milk well, and will usually show their intolerance by a bout of diarrhoea within hours of drinking it. Rice pudding, which is a good food for invalids and puppies, can be made with evaporated milk, which dogs love and it never upsets them. If, for reasons best known to yourself,

you simply must give milk to your dog, then ensure it is semi-skimmed.

### Treats

Dog lovers are notorious for their need to give 'extras' to their pets. Many owners would not dream of going to bed without giving their dog a final treat, and frequently a treat is given to dogs when the owner leaves the house. The greatest use of treats is as a reward for good behaviour. I never walk my dogs without having titbits in my pocket, as this ensures their swift return when called: without the treats, they develop selective deafness!

When feeding treats we should not underestimate the bulk, and calories, which they add to the dog's daily rations. A poster in my vet's surgery clearly illustrates just how much of an 'extra' a biscuit can be: the illustration shows an owner handing a dog a large dog biscuit, but there is a thought bubble above the dog's head showing a double cheeseburger – in other words, a treat which seems relatively small to us, is viewed as a relatively substantial offering by the dog!

There are low-calorie treats, but read the pack before giving these as some are of much higher calorific value than others.

### Bones

To feed or not to feed bones has been a continuing argument for years. There are people who feed a diet of raw chicken wings to their dogs (and even to young puppies), but a conversation with most vets will reveal details of long and complicated operations where splinters have perforated the gut. However, devotees of feeding this way are quite passionate about what they do, and I have no intention of becoming embroiled in an argument. I mention this diet merely because it exists.

The only bones I use are the white, chalky, sterilized type, and I always use the hollow ones, although many are sold with a meat or cheese filling. My rationale for not using these is that they are sold from heated shops, and such fillings need to be refrigerated if they are not to become a breeding ground for bacteria. On occasions when the unfilled type is not available, I buy the filled ones, remove the filling and boil them to scald – and so destroy – anything unpleasant that might be lurking.

These chalky bones do not shatter like the smoked variety, which are all too often baked at high temperatures, making them excessively brittle. A useful way to occupy a dog when leaving him unattended is to fill the bone with moistened bread, into which small pieces of biscuit meal and cheese have been hidden. Squeeze the mixture and pack it into the bone with the handle of a wooden spoon, and the dog will have hours of fun trying to get it out.

This is a very useful way of distracting dogs that have just had an operation and would like to remove their bandages; giving a home-filled bone makes the wearing of the large plastic 'lampshade' collar unnecessary.

Plastic cubes and balls are available, with a reservoir into which small treats can be concealed; the dog pushes the toy around, and every so often a treat will fall out. However, be sure only to use such toys with one dog, as two or more could easily disagree in the excitement of the moment as the food pieces appear. Dogs do not need variety in the same way that humans need to vary what they eat: once you have found a food that your dog likes and which keeps him in good condition, stay with it.

## Choosing a Food Product

### Is Dearest the Best?

It is tempting to believe that very expensive foods are better for your dog, and it is an interesting exercise to compare the ingredients' panels that are printed on the side of dog food bags. I used to stand in the shop with rows of bags, carefully making notes on each; however, Internet access now makes this possible in the comfort of your own home. Note especially how much sugar-beet pulp is in some foods: it is a filler, and produces very large, bulky stools. Also notice the oil content: I prefer this to be relatively high (7 per cent or over) as Goldens do need it to maintain a glossy coat, especially the paler dogs whose coat tends to be dry.

### Gluten or Gluten Free?

I would choose the gluten-free range every time, as gluten is a source of digestive upset in humans and dogs. Why feed it when the presence of gluten may cause problems and its absence definitely will not? Note that dog snacks may also contain gluten, or they may be gluten free. It is not only dry foods that may have gluten content, but tinned foods also.

### What Flavour is Best?

The best flavour is the one your dog finds most palatable. There are dogs that will eat any food, irrespective of flavour. I have dogs that are upset by chicken-flavoured foods, yet they can eat those flavoured with turkey or duck. It is worth noting just what percentage of poultry is actually present, because in some foods it is substantially higher.

The meat considered to be the most hypoallergenic is lamb, and few dogs have an intolerance to it. I always use a lamb and gluten-free diet for the dogs in Golden Retriever Rescue as it never seems to upset them.

## Feeding Dishes

Whichever dish you choose it must withstand being scalded to keep it clean. Avoid plastic bowls, as Goldens are notorious for throwing these around and for chewing them. Also, as dogs eat, grooves develop in plastic, and bacteria will congregate into these. Ceramic or stainless-steel dishes are the preferred choice.

*There will be one style of dish to suit every dog.*

The downside of the former is that they are heavy, and even more so if used as water bowls; they also break and crack if dropped. Stainless steel is light and easy to keep clean, but dents easily and makes a noise on tiled floors.

It was said earlier that dogs do not require variety in their food, and to stay with what suited them – but there is no virtue in offering the same food if the dog is obviously sick and tired of it. When you change food, do so over a period of at least a week, or digestive upsets will occur.

## Water

It is essential for all dogs to have unlimited access to fresh, cold water. Water standing in metal dishes becomes very warm indeed if left in the sun. Goldens dig a lot, and so the first drink they have after an 'excavating' episode frequently leaves deposits of soil in the bowl; as a result you will have to change their water frequently. This is even more important if you have two dogs, otherwise the second dog will have to drink dirty water.

If you take your dog away from home, take a supply of your own water with you. If you travel on hot days, freeze a large plastic bottle of water, and only remove it from the freezer as you set off; it will thaw slowly and remain cooler for longer. Alternatively you could take water in one of the freezer bags now available.

# 6 Breeding

The first question that needs to be addressed before you embark on breeding a litter is why you actually want to do so. If the reason is that you want a puppy, then you will need to consider whether the enormous amount of effort, time and expense entailed is really your best option, when the alternative is to go to a reputable breeder and buy one. Frequently, the reason given for breeding is that it is 'good for the bitch to have a litter'; however, there are thousands of perfectly happy, well adjusted bitches that have never been bred from, and I have no reason to believe their lives would have been further enhanced by producing puppies.

## Points for Consideration

The expense of raising a litter is no small consideration. Stud fees are rising, and at this time you should expect to pay at least £600 if you want to mate your bitch to a champion male. There is, of course, the expense of purchasing your bitch in the first place, rearing her until she is mature enough to be bred from, and then the not inconsiderable cost of registering and feeding the litter. If you add all these together, just getting started in the serious business of breeding is going to cost you in excess of £2,000. You must also ensure that you have suffcient funds should veterinary intervention, such as a Caesarean

*The expense of raising a litter is no small consideration.*

section, be needed, or should the puppies become ill.

Further factors to consider include deciding whether you have suffcient time and dedication to be at home with mother and puppies for at least eight weeks. It is incredibly time-consuming to care for a bitch and her litter. In the first instance, the puppies need to be watched around the clock to ensure the dam doesn't inadvertently lie on one or more; this is particularly important in the hours following whelping when she is exhausted. Responsible breeders sleep with them for the first three weeks, after which time the puppies are generally able to get out of the way if the bitch threatens to squash them; they are also suffciently vocal to alert her before accidents occur.

Once weaning starts, you need to be present for their four feeds, which should be given at the same time each day. This encroaches on your time, and any social life you might have had before the litter arrived, is indefinitely on hold.

The most time-consuming part of coping with a litter is when prospective owners come to view: you allow an hour for each visitor, but most stay for double that time or longer. They seem to bring all their relations, so your role alternates between that of dog breeder and of waitress.

## The Brood Bitch

If you have carefully considered all these points and are adamant about wanting to breed Golden Retrievers, then your first consideration is acquiring a bitch that will provide your foundation litter.

Even if you already have a bitch, she isn't necessarily the most suitable animal to breed from. The most important thing to consider is temperament, and then comes freedom from inherited defects: both your bitch, and the dog you choose to mate her to, should have the most perfect temperament imaginable, and should be reliable with children, adults and other dogs. If there is any

*You will require a sound, typical bitch to produce your first litter.*

*Temperament of all breeding stock is of prime importance.*

deviation from this, then it is imperative you do *not* go ahead with your breeding plans.

Each one of the puppies you produce must live in society in a well adjusted manner. So great is the media coverage of every dog that steps out of line, that you and the puppies you produce could face very expensive legal action if things go wrong. We live in a highly litigious environment, and should be aware of this throughout plans to breed. If a dog you breed bites someone and legal proceedings result, at least you, as the breeder, are on more secure ground if you prove that the sire and dam have impeccable temperaments. If either one is suspect, so will be the outcome of legal investigations.

Inherited defects are discussed in detail elsewhere, but before she is bred from your bitch must be hip x-rayed and scored, and that score must fall under the average for the breed. Her eyes must be tested annually, and the certificate of clearance should be current at the time of mating. Do not bury your head in the sand and think it doesn't matter if the hip score is rather high as you are only intending to breed pets and not show dogs. Pets have the right to a healthy, pain-free life, too. Owners should expect to buy a puppy

that has been bred in a wholly responsible way, and not one produced as a result of cutting corners.

Do not fall into the trap of going ahead with your breeding programme if your bitch passes her eye test on all but one of the inherited conditions. It could be this very one that causes blindness in future litters.

If the bitch you already have fails on any of the above criteria, then keep her as a much-loved pet but discard her from any future breeding plans. Do not view her as a waste of space, however, because valuable lessons are to be learned from such failures. Even the most famous breeder with a string of champions to her reputation is likely to have had such a bitch initially.

**Buying a Brood Bitch**

If you set out to buy a bitch specifically for breeding when she is old enough, be honest and tell the breeder what you want. It helps if you have a clear idea of what you want before you approach breeders, so that you and they share common aims. Do your homework before you think of buying. Go to shows, study pedigrees and find out not only who produces the most winning dogs, but who produces the soundest stock. Results of hip and eye examinations are freely available for you to study. Beware of the breeder who only ever produces good stock for herself. The mark of a truly good breeder is one who regularly produces sound, typical stock for complete novices. Talk to novice owners who have bought from breeders who interest you.

Eventually, narrow your chosen kennels to two or three, and ask to visit these breeders. Breeders who are also exhibitors are busy people, so do not expect to be made welcome the day before a show when dogs are being prepared, or (even worse) if you turn up unannounced.

Go with a list of questions, because in the excitement of the visit you will be unlikely to remember everything you want to know. If you cannot think of a list, the following should help:

1. Which bitch(es) will be bred from next?
2. Has she had litters before?
3. What was the hip and eye status of those puppies?
4. What is the hip and eye status of her litter mates?
5. Can I make a fuss of this bitch?
6. Is either of her parents here? Can I see them?
7. Are your puppies reared in the house or out in a kennel?
8. Do you consider novice owners for your puppies, and if so, would you consider me?
9. What would I pay for one of your puppies?
10. At what age do you let your puppies go to their new homes?

If one or more bitches will be bred from, ask the breeder's advice on which would make the best foundation bitch for you. Be guided by what they say, but view what they say in the light of the knowledge you have gained so far. Be aware that some breeders are very skilled in the art of making a sale!

One question I always ask is, what will happen if the puppy I have chosen does not fulfil the criteria for which she has been bought? The breeder's answer to this will tell you a great deal about their commitment, responsibility and professionalism.

When I am asked this, I reply that should the puppy have a hip score too high for breeding, or if she should fail an eye test, I will reimburse the full purchase price. I have stuck to this premise rigidly throughout forty-two years of breeding, and am happy to say I have only had to honour it twice.

Be extremely wary of the breeder who, on being asked this question, goes off into lengthy explanations which all boil down to the answer, 'You've paid your money and you take your chance.' They will also talk about there being no guarantee: of course there can't be a guarantee, but there should be a responsible and fair commitment to the live animal produced.

As a breeder, you will also have to ensure you are in a position to take back any failures you breed. If you are not in a position to do so, do not breed. What is important when choosing a bitch to breed from is that not only her parents but animals further back in the pedigree were sound. As many of them will no longer be living, you will have to rely on records and information from others who remember that far back. Kennel jealousy exists among breeders, so be suspicious of the breeder who finds nothing good to say about any stock unless she bred it.

One factor that should not influence your decision is price, but remember the dearest is not necessarily the best, nor the cheapest the worst. There has always been secrecy surrounding what certain kennels charge, and rumours abound, but the sure way to find out is to ask the breeder directly and avoid asking others, who might greatly distort the truth.

Areas affect cost, and frequently prices will vary greatly according to the part of Britain in which the puppies are bred. It's a fair comment that if this puppy is really what you want, then it is worth the asking price.

It is unlikely that all ten puppies in a litter will be the most superb specimens ever produced, but it is reasonable to expect a proportion of them to be good. I work by the rule of thirds, so in a litter of nine I would expect three to be very good, three to be average and three to be less good. This is by no means infallible, as it is possible to have litters where the majority has gone on to do very well in the show ring throughout the world. Conversely I have had litters, beautifully bred

*Good breeding should produce good puppies.*

from generations of champions, that were mediocre. Some matings work and some do not.

You will now have made the decision whether your existing bitch is to be the dam of your future litter, or if it is to be the one you have bought in specially. Nothing is so unpredictable as breeding, so be prepared for disappointments along the way. If you are stronger as a result and absolutely determined to breed a litter, then you deserve to succeed.

At the time of mating your bitch should be in peak condition, and definitely should not be fat. Such condition isn't reached quickly, so the year leading up to the planned mating should be used to get her in good condition.

When to breed is a question about which much has been written, and even more discussed. I favour the season after the bitch is two and a half years old, because bitches of this age generally whelp easily, and rearing a litter takes less out of them than it does out of older bitches.

## Choosing a Stud Dog

You will know for at least a year roughly when you will mate your bitch, so use that year to look at males in the show ring, and follow the progress of the progeny of dogs you like. Also check that your preferred males are producing sound, typical stock with lovely temperaments. It is not suffcient for the dogs to win: they must also be healthy and happy.

It makes sense to choose dogs that look like your bitch as well as having related animals in their pedigrees. If you choose a dog from totally different lines, this is known as 'outcrossing' and has several drawbacks: first and foremost is the fact that when two unrelated, or only distantly related, animals are mated together, you have no idea what will result. Whereas if you mate animals of common ancestors together, then you can predict with a degree of accuracy what will result.

View with great scepticism all the tales you have heard of the dangers of in-breeding. You will hear that in-bred dogs produce bad hips and eyes – but if this were true, the fact that

*The stud dog should look typical and be free from inherited defects.*

mongrels also produce the same problems would be diffcult to explain. It is also blamed for bad temperament: again, if this were true, all mongrels and cross-breeds should have the perfect temperament.

## In-Breeding

In-breeding is the term used to denote the mating of closely related animals, such as half-brother and sister, or mother to son. The advantage is that because the animals are so similar in type, you can predict with accuracy how the puppies will look. The disadvantage is that if any inherited defects are lurking, which have not actually made themselves known previously, they will have been doubled, quadrupled and more, so laying down a store of problems for this, and future, generations.

In-breeding should only be undertaken by breeders who have many years of experience, and who knew personally the majority of the dogs in the pedigrees of both the dog and bitch. Such breeding should never be attempted by novices.

It is always important only to breed from animals with the soundest temperament, but with in-breeding this factor becomes vitally important, as every aspect of the parents' characters will be doubled.

I have in-bred with great success, producing champions by this method. My personal considerations, before mating the intended animals together, include not only the temperament factor discussed above, but how sound and typical of the breed they are. They must also be as free from inherited defects as possible, nor should they possess any exaggerations. For example, if you were to in-breed with two short-legged animals, which also happened to have short-legged parents, then it should come as no surprise to find the resulting puppies had short, or even shorter, legs. Nothing would have been gained by such a mating, and surely the aim must be to improve with each generation produced.

## Out-Crossing

Sometimes using a slight outcross parent has to be done when dogs have been closely bred to one line over a period of time. These matings have results which are impossible to predict, and often disappoint. My personal experience is that while such matings can produce individuals that are of excellent type and conformation, they themselves seldom produce the desired type in future generations.

Out-crossing, by definition, is using a dog that has completely different lines from your bitch. If you use such a dog because you would like one just like him, then you will be disappointed because the resulting puppies will have a mixture of the characteristics of the many animals in both parents' pedigrees. It is not possible to select the bits you require and discard those you do not; breeding is simply not that easy.

## Producing Sound Stock

To produce sound, typical stock you need to be aware of the virtues and failings of both parents (and ideally of their parents), and avoid extremes. For example, never mate a bitch that is fine in the head to a heavy-headed male: you will not get the ideal of halfway between the two, but will get some of each, neither of which is desirable. To correct a fine-headed bitch, you would choose a dog with a correct, well balanced head.

Never breed for one aspect alone, because if this does not correct itself you will probably not gain in any of the other areas, either.

Avoid first-time stud dogs because they are sometimes diffcult to mate to maiden bitches; and also, there will be no progeny that you can look at, to see if that dog is producing what you require. It is safer to go for older dogs, because by then any undesired

traits in their progeny would have manifested themselves. To illustrate this point, there was a stunning, top winner many years ago, and by the time he was just over a year old and his hip score and eye-test results were known, there was a queue of beautifully bred bitches waiting for him. Many litters were produced, and they looked most promising; and as they became old enough to be shown, they won really well. And then the sire was diagnosed with epilepsy, and many of those lovely youngsters fell foul of this most awful complaint. Had some breeders waited a while, the condition would have shown itself, and so many litters would not have resulted. We cannot play God as breeders, but it pays to be cautious.

Stud dogs of five and upwards, which have a lot of stock around, are the safest bet. Nothing is foolproof, but some risks can be reduced. Some conditions do have a late onset, but such instances are really unfortunate and relatively rare. All dogs and bitches will, if used often enough, produce a few undesirable results. That is the way breeding goes, and it is hard to accept and devastating when it happens. Breeding is definitely not for the faint-hearted! One incredibly successful breeder abroad remarked 'All animals have the potential to produce disasters. Accept it and when it occurs, do the best possible things for the welfare of that animal, then move on.' Very sound advice, but the moving on is sometimes hard to take.

## Recognizing Signs of Oestrus

Once you have chosen your stud dog, alert the owner to the fact that you would like to use him, and give a rough idea when you expect your bitch to be in season. Remember to *request*, and not demand to use him, or you'll get off on the wrong foot!

Your bitch will exhibit signs of coming into season before she actually starts. Bitches will 'mark' by urinating small quantities instead of the one large puddle they usually produce. It is not unusual for them to 'mark' throughout a walk. Male dogs will sniff the bitch interestedly and will refuse to come away from the 'marked' sites, their teeth chattering as they investigate. Bitches about to come in season (also called 'heat' and 'oestrus') will have an enlarged vulva, which they will clean vigorously after urinating.

The first day of the season proper is when the discharge is bloody. Often this is a slightly rusty colour as it begins, but within hours it changes to bright red. This red discharge will persist for up to twelve days, when the intensity will subside and it will become straw-coloured. This, coupled with a softer vulva and a tendency to twitch her tail to one side, are all signals that she is ready for mating.

Some bitches have a few false starts before the season really begins, which can be confusing. If, after the initial discharge, nothing is visible for several days, count from the day the bloody discharge reappears.

At this time the bitch is frantic to mate other bitches, and care should be taken, as not all bitches are receptive to such overtures, and heated disagreements are possible. Some bitches show a desire to play sexually motivated games all through their season, so this is not always a reliable guide to the correct day for mating them.

It is customary to inform the stud dog owner of the first day your bitch comes in season, as top dogs are generally in demand, and it is often a question of juggling to arrange that no two bitches come on the same day. Any stud dog owner will tell you that you can have weeks of inactivity, then all the bitches appear to be ready on the same day. This week, as I write, three bitches are booked to my dog, and all appear to be nearing the optimum time at the same rate! Luckily we now have blood-testing, which pinpoints the exact day the bitch should be mated, so I'm hoping that three different dates result!

## Mating Day

For novice owners (and for many who are more experienced), the tests that vets perform now take all the guesswork out of mating. However, my preferred method is to let my dogs tell me the exact day the bitches are ready, as they never get it wrong. For people without a resident and experienced male, the answer is the blood test. Contact your vet on day one of your bitch's season, and he will guide you from there. Generally, the results will show that you have several days, at least two or three, to do the mating, but a small percentage of bitches do not follow this rule. Some will be ready and over within a day, and a few will be ready for about a week. I have always worked to the premise that if my dog tells me the bitch is ready on one day, then I take her to the stud dog the following day, and I have never had a bitch fail to produce a litter by this method.

If you are having blood tests for your bitch, keep the stud dog's owner informed of the progress throughout. There is nothing more irritating than being told on day one of the bitch's season that she is to be blood-tested, then hearing nothing until the phone rings to tell you that bitch and owner are at the nearest motorway services and will be with you soon as the bitch is ready to be mated that morning.

### Introducing the Dog and Bitch

Bitches that live alone and are not used to other dogs are often quite overwhelmed on first meeting the stud dog. Both animals should be on a lead, and should meet in a quiet, escape-proof place such as a garage or fenced exercise run. This area should be large enough to accommodate both dogs and their handlers, but not so large that, when the animals play freely, the owners cannot instantly catch them.

Ensure that the bitch is rested after a long journey, and that she has a chance to relieve herself before attempting the mating. Having permitted them to meet while still on leads, you will gain a fairly accurate idea of how she responds to the male. If she shows indications of flirting, remove the leads and let them play; this has a twofold benefit in that it relaxes the bitch and makes her more receptive to the dog's advances.

If she shows no resistance when the dog mounts, move quietly in and hold her collar, having first ensured it is tight enough not to slip off if she jerks her head. Just hold tightly, and the stud dog owner will organize everything at the important end. Remember, you are at the sharp end and even the best tempered bitches may snap, and even bite, if they become frightened.

A muzzle is essential for a bitch that is determined to bite her owner or the dog. If she shows aggression when introduced to the dog, that is the time to muzzle her.

### What Actually Happens?
The dog will mount, and after several thrusts will fully penetrate the bitch. The dog will ejaculate, and a bulb of erectile tissue swells. A strong muscle ring in the bitch's vagina will grip the dog, and he will remain tied to the bitch for anything up to an hour. Matings last anything from fifteen to ninety minutes, although thirty is a fair average.

Once the dog ties, he will remain inert on the bitch's back for a few seconds, and then he will usually drop down to one side of the bitch, where he will remain until the tie ends. A few stud dogs will turn back to back with the bitch, but I never encourage this because such a position is harder to handle.

The bitch's owner must hold her firmly until the tie comes to an end, preventing her from pulling away or attempting to lie down.

If she has been muzzled it should be removed once the dog has dismounted, provided she shows no signs of aggression.

The surface on which the mating takes place is important as animals that are slipping and sliding will not mate confidently. Rubber-backed mats are ideal, as is rough concrete or dry grass. Very short bitches can be elevated on several thicknesses of carpet, or can be mated on a slope (so that the hindquarters are higher than the head).

Once the mating has taken place, the bitch and dog should be offered a drink and put into separate cool, quiet places while their owners do the paperwork.

### Important Paperwork
The stud dog's owner will have inspected the bitch's certificates of hip scores and eye status before the mating. Afterwards the stud dog's owner will give copies of these certificates to the bitch's owner, along with a copy of his pedigree. A photograph of the dog is not obligatory, but most owners are glad of this to show to future puppy buyers. Also, a signed litter registration form will be handed to the bitch's owner, with details of the stud dog, his owner's details and the date of mating. Once the litter is born, the owner will complete the form, choose names for the puppies, and send this with the required fee to the Kennel Club.

Breeders may apply for an affx, a word that will be used in front of each puppy's name. My own affx is 'Linchael', therefore on the litter registration form for the litters I breed, each puppy would have this word as the start of its whole name, such as 'Linchael Diva'. Only those to whom the affx has been granted may use this word, and an annual maintenance fee must be paid to the Kennel Club.

If you intend registering your own affx, do so well in advance of the mating because it takes quite a while for your application to be processed and the affx granted. When choosing an affx, avoid names in your bitch's pedigree as these will be owned by other breeders. Many affxes are a mix of the owners' names, or are the names of their children (try taking two letters from husband, wife and children, and see what words are formed), or relate to addresses or characteristics of the breed.

## Care of the In-whelp Bitch

For the first few weeks of her pregnancy the bitch will require nothing different from usual, provided she is fed on a good quality food. From halfway through her pregnancy, she will need special care.

If you are not sure whether she is in whelp or not, you can have her scanned at twenty-eight days, a non-invasive procedure lasting a couple of minutes. A picture of the uterus appears on the screen and outlines of puppies may (not very clearly) be seen. It is diffcult to see puppies lying behind others, so if four are visible, it is possible she may be carrying eight.

I never have mine scanned as I enjoy the anticipation of whether or not my bitch is in whelp. I usually know by her behaviour, long before there are visible signs. My bitches will slow down immediately they are mated; they refrain from tearing through the field gate with the others, and they decline any attempts to make them play. Generally, they appear to be taking care of themselves.

I do not take my in-whelp bitches in the car unless it is absolutely unavoidable, and then I use a ramp to prevent them jumping in and out. Try to avoid going to the vet's surgery with an in-whelp bitch: this is where sick dogs go, and the last thing you want is for her to contract any infection. Call the vet to your house if you need him, and ask him to remove his shoes before entering the house, so reducing the spread of any infection. A former vet of mine once remarked that he wouldn't have been at all surprised if

I'd hosed him down on the doorstep and then insisted he walked in on his hands! One can't be too careful!

Once you know your bitch is pregnant, she will need a richer diet than she has formerly been fed. I change the adult complete diet to one made for puppies, as this will have the required nutrients. She will have an increasing need for protein, vitamins, minerals and energy-giving ingredients (carbohydrates). Do not be tempted to give calcium supplements, as this can interfere with the natural availability of calcium in the body during lactation, and the dreaded eclampsia (discussed in detail later, *see* page 132) could result.

She will be eating a complete diet, usually having an approximately 28 per cent protein content, for the last four weeks of her pregnancy. I also give raw meat, not the pet-mince type, but real butcher's meat, and I also give two eggs a day.

As the bitch increases in size, so her capacity for accepting large meals will diminish. If she is uncomfortably full on two meals a day, divide these into three or four. Be sensible, and compare it with the unlikely event of a heavily pregnant woman finding it acceptable to eat a five-course meal.

## Preparation before Whelping Day

You will need to buy or make a whelping box. This is a 4ft (1.2m) square bed with three sides higher than the fourth; ideally it should be constructed so the sides can be raised as the puppies grow, to stop them abseiling over the sides.

Wood should be coated with several layers of non-toxic gloss paint. Never use any sort of wood preservative, which is highly toxic.

Guard-rails to stop puppies getting squashed are fixed to the sides. Broom handles are ideal, and these can be slotted through holes at the corners of the box. The Internet is laden with

*A home-made whelping box.*

sites of companies selling whelping boxes, but these run into hundreds of pounds, and unless you are intending having many litters, are very expensive. They are, however, beautifully made, and many take apart for easy storage.

Some people use the new coated cardboard disposable birthing boxes. I have never used one, but have heard good reports from those who have. Nevertheless, for the price of one of these, a wooden one can be made at home which will last for many years – the one my bitches whelp in was made thirty-five years ago and shows no signs of wear; it is scrubbed thoroughly after use, and has a couple of coats of gloss paint before it is needed again.

Do not expect your bitch just to hop into the box and whelp on the appointed day. Introduce her to it weeks in advance, and if she is reluctant to step into it, use it as a feeding station. Few bitches mind where they eat, and this should accustom her to her new surroundings. On several occasions I have sat down and read a book in the whelping box to persuade bitches that it is a pleasant, secure place to be. Give her a thick bed while she is getting used to the box, and as the day approaches, she will usually make a 'nest' from this.

You will need a few items for the birth itself. I have clean towels and a large quantity of wet-wipes for my hands. Blunt-ended scissors are used if the bitch is reluctant to bite the umbilical cord. I have a couple of large plastic bags which I use for soiled towels and used wipes. A flask of coffee is essential for the exhausted owner, and another of glucose and water for the bitch. Several clean, fleecy-type blankets will be needed, and stacks of clean newspapers for putting between this and the box. Whelping is a very wet affair, with more liquid arriving with the birth of each puppy. You will also need pen and paper to record the time of birth as each puppy arrives.

A week before the litter is due, I trim off all the feathering on the bitch's tail and the feathering on her back legs. This is to minimize the quantity of mess resulting from the natural discharge occurring after birth. This

*A commercially available box.*

can continue for a fortnight, and the walls and doorways of your house will really suffer if your bitch is not trimmed – with each movement of her tail, more splashes occur. Another reason for this trimming is that thick wet fur makes the bitch really sore, and a sort of nappy rash will result. If the fur is trimmed, you can wash and dry her rear end several times a day. My bitches just accept being backed into the shower and having a quick rinse. The trimmed fur takes little drying, and towelling is all that is needed. Furthermore, if you leave all the feathering on, the resulting odour from the discharge is unpleasant and diffcult to live with in a household situation.

## Puppy Day Arrives

I am frequently asked, 'Will I know when she is about to whelp?' Oh yes, you'll know! The most reliable sign is that her temperature will drop within twenty-four hours of whelping. She will usually refuse food within twelve hours of starting to whelp – although I have vivid memories of a bitch eating a hearty meal and finishing just in time to jump into the whelping box and produce her first puppy! All signs are general, but your bitch could always be the exception.

For a week or two before whelping, many bitches dig large holes in the garden (or carpet!). They will try to tunnel under sheds and garages, and must be prevented from getting in so deeply that you cannot get them out. This digging persists with many bitches, even after the litter has been born. It does no harm, but the downside is that they tread soil back into their beds.

The first stage of whelping is the temperature drop, then comes frantic bed making. As soon as whelping proper begins, the bitch has a glazed expression, seeing past you and what is familiar, to the task beyond. It is now that she will have contractions, and as she does so, she will grunt and arch her back. This is sometimes quite quickly followed by the birth of the first puppy, but generally at least an hour of contractions is needed before the first puppy emerges.

*This puppy has just been born.*

Ideally he should be born head first with paws each side, emerging from the vulva with each contraction. If he appears stuck, grip gently but firmly around the shoulders, using a towel, as he will slip from your bare hands, and pull in a downward motion with each contraction. He will either emerge in or out of the sac, which looks like a plastic bag. If the sac is around his head, break it with your fingernails; there is no feeling in this membrane, so you will hurt neither bitch nor puppy. There will be a rush of fluid as you puncture this sac. The puppy will be born attached to an irregular liver-looking mass, the placenta. Allow the bitch to eat it unless it is green, when you'll have to be very smart to get it before she does. Again, use a towel to pick it up or it will just slither from your grasp.

As each puppy arrives, those already born will get wet unless you move them. I have a hot-water bottle (well covered, so there is no chance of it burning them) in a corner of the whelping box, and I move the puppies on to this, in view of their mother, who would become distressed if they were to 'disappear'. I also have a cardboard box outside the whelping box, complete with covered hot-water bottle. This is in case the bitch becomes too animated as she whelps and in danger of treading on, or lying on, those in the corner.

If a puppy seems slow to breathe immediately after birth, rub it vigorously with a

*Ensure that each puppy is feeding well.*

towel, holding it with its head downhill to drain fluid from the lungs. And if it is still reluctant to breathe, swing it gently, with its head down. This often clears the lungs and the motion encourages the intake of breath.

Most puppies find their own way to their mother's teats, but there is the occasional simpleton who wanders off in the opposite direction, yelling loudly because he's lost his way. Return puppies who wander to the 'milk bar'.

## When to Get Help

Most Goldens are very easy whelpers, albeit rather slow; and the longer they take over the process, the more exhausted they become. If the bitch goes beyond her due date by three days, the vet is needed.

If the bitch strains vigorously (as distinct from the half-hearted movements made at the start of whelping) for over an hour, then veterinary intervention is needed. Some bitches will whelp half of their litter, then stop, with no further signs of puppies emerging. This is known as inertia, and a veterinary injection usually gets everything going again.

If a puppy is visibly stuck and no amount of pushing by the bitch or tugging by you makes any difference, then the vet will be needed.

Any odd behaviour exhibited by the bitch in the days following whelping should be viewed with suspicion. She could have retained a dead puppy, or could be starting the dreaded eclampsia (*see* page 132). Either condition, left untreated, would cause the death of the bitch, and most likely that of her litter.

## After Whelping

A newly whelped bitch will be desperate to go outside to relieve herself, but will be frantic at the thought of leaving her litter. She will need to be taken outside on the lead or she will run back to the puppies, without 'going'.

When you take her out, take a torch with you, as there are many records of bitches who, when straining to relieve themselves, push out a puppy. There have been sad cases where inexperienced breeders have found a dead puppy in the garden next morning. The torch is essential.

While you are out with her, someone else should remove the soiled bedding from the whelping box, then dry the surface, and place thick newspaper on the bottom and a thick rug on top. Ensure that the soiled bedding is well out of the bitch's sight and smell when she returns, or she will obsessively search through it, believing you have hidden some of her babies.

Each time I take my bitches out, I wipe their underparts with a damp cloth, then dry them before they return to their litters. This ensures that nothing is sticking to the teats, which could harm the pups.

If the bitch has eaten one or more afterbirths she will feel pretty full, and only a drink will be required. You will need to hold the water bowl in the whelping box for her to drink, as she will certainly not leave the box to do so. Never leave it in the box or puppies could drown. Honey and glucose mixed with water is welcomed by the tired mother. Next morning offer her a light meal of boiled fish and rice, or chicken and rice.

Her water intake will increase markedly as she produces more milk for her litter.

Repeat this meal three or four times a day. Eating the placentas causes the bitch's motions to be loose, and the rice helps with the production of firmer stools.

*The chalky tips of puppies' nails must be clipped regularly.*

*The bitch needs to be able to get away from the litter.*

By the fourth day after whelping, your bitch will be ready to return to her normal diet, mixed in equal quantities with the fish and rice. By the end of the week, leave out the fish/chicken and rice, and allow her to return to her usual eating habits. My yardstick for quantities is that if she's eating it all, appears satisfied, and doesn't have diarrhoea, then the quantity must be right.

For as long as the bitch is discharging, you will need to wash her rear end several times a day. Failure to do this will result in a sore bitch that is in too much discomfort to permit her litter to suckle. Use a very mild baby shampoo as the puppies will be in close contact with this area, and anything stronger would upset them.

Make sure the puppies are feeding from all the teats, or those not being emptied will become hard and painful, and mastitis could result. Also, ensure the tips of the pups' nails (these appear chalky white) are trimmed, or they will make their mother very sore. Do not cut beyond this chalky part or bleeding will result.

The bitch must always be able to get away from her puppies. From the second week most bitches will lie at the side of the box, only going in to feed and lie with the babies at night. Extra care is needed when the bitch first enters the box, as there is a danger of some puppies getting underneath their mother as she lies down. By the end of the third week, I take the front off the box so that the pups can wander further afield; they cannot be absolutely free or they would go too far from the box. A puppy pen should be erected around the box, constructed from panels of mesh that bolt together. A door is incorporated on to one side to permit free access by the breeder.

Newspapers should be put down in one corner of the run so that the puppies can start toilet training. It is amazing how quickly they learn to keep their bed clean.

## The Lactating Bitch

As the bitch produces more and more milk, so she will need more food, and copious quantities of water. As long as she has suffcient milk, the puppies will sleep contentedly between each feed. Be watchful that each puppy gets an equal share, and if your bitch has fewer teats than she has puppies, you must ensure all take turns at feeding and that you supplement the feeds by bottle feeding. Powdered feed is sold specifically for this purpose.

The bitch's motions will be a guide to her state of health. After whelping she will pass black, evil-smelling faeces as a result of eating the afterbirths; by day three, these should return to normal. There will be a change in the consistency once she is cleaning up after the puppies, and even more so once you are feeding them several meals a day, so causing them to produce even more waste.

## Weaning the Puppies

Pups will have everything they require when they feed from their dams for the first few weeks. The first milk they take is known as colostrum, and is vital for their well-being, and essential if they are to develop a healthy immune system. Should they not have access to this colostrum, then the powdered variety must be administered by syringe (minus the needle).

By three weeks the pups are ready for their first feed given by the breeder. Tiny balls of raw mince should be rolled in the palm of your hand and offered to individual pups. For

*Puppy porridge is introduced.*

*Weaning puppies is a messy business.*

a second they hesitate, unsure of what they must do. But suddenly the penny drops, and after that moment they are never unsure again! After a few days of offering raw meat twice a day, puppy porridge should be introduced: this is bought in powdered form and is mixed with water. At first this mixture is given as the consistency of thin custard, but once the puppies are lapping well, the mixture can be thicker.

Weaning puppies is a messy business, and you are advised to have a wet flannel and much kitchen roll for the operation. Dip each pup's nose into the mixture, and after a few attempts they will start lapping.

By five weeks, the breeder will be offering four or five meals a day, and the bitch will be permitted to give them a late night drink, for as long as she has milk and is willing to feed them. Sometimes the pups just become too much for her and she will refuse to feed them, but by then her milk should dry naturally; however, check her teats regularly to see there is no hardness.

## Worming

Puppies must be wormed regularly, as there is no point in providing first class food which is feeding the worms at the expense of the puppy. Furthermore, a heavy worm burden in young puppies can be fatal. They should be wormed from two weeks of age, with the dose repeated every two weeks until they are three months old. Obtain worming preparations from the veterinary surgery, resisting the urge to buy such drugs over the counter in pet shops.

## Parasites

It is essential to spray the puppies for cheyletiella (mange mites). These have the common name of 'walking dandruff', because that is exactly how they look. They are highly

irritant, and a spray with a preparation obtained from your vet will put an end to the infestation.

Isolate each puppy, brush the fur up with your hand, and allow the fine spray to penetrate the fur. Avoid the eyes and nostrils, and take care not to inhale the spray yourself. Pat the coat of each puppy dry before returning it to its litter mates, and do not permit the dam to lick the puppies.

*Young puppies may be bathed in the kitchen sink.*

I always bath my puppies before they go to their new homes, so ensure you bath before you spray them, otherwise all will be washed away. To bath puppies, use the kitchen sink with just a couple of inches of tepid water, and have the puppy shampoo (avoid using those for adults) ready mixed in a jug. Place a non-slip mat in the sink, and another on the draining board. The second mat is covered

*Dry initially with a towel.*

with a towel. Puppies sometimes panic as you lower them into the water, so it is important to do everything calmly, reassuring them with your voice. Having shampooed and rinsed well, I pat off the worst of the water with a towel. I dry with a hair dryer if the puppy accepts it (on the lowest temperature), or with towels. It is a very rewarding sight, to see your carefully planned litter spotlessly clean and ready to go.

# 7 Having Fun With Your Dog

All dogs benefit if they have something to occupy their minds, and the Golden Retriever is no exception. It doesn't matter what he is given to do, as long as he is given something. The possibilities are endless, and range from basic obedience and simple tricks to advanced gundog work. None of this need be competitive, but there is no doubt that training and competing in the company of others is mutually beneficial.

The majority of exercises are more easily taught to a puppy, but this is not exclusively so. In fact, in a few instances some activities would be detrimental to a young dog: agility is one such discipline, where it would be positively injurious to a puppy's joints, with all the jumping involved. All strenuous activities should only be attempted by dogs in perfect health. If you have any doubts, consult your vet before beginning the dog's training.

All healthy Goldens are capable of learning new skills, but the level of that learning varies greatly with the individual. Never expect the speed and precision of the Border Collie, or you will be disappointed – though having said that, the slimmer, working type of Golden is quite fast. It is a case of 'horses for courses', and you will possibly try several activities before you find one that suits you both. To give an example, I have a very sweet and gentle three-year-old bitch that is my absolute shadow, but I don't show her, and I felt she needed some sort of stimulus. I tried several activities until I hit on the idea of teaching her

*Training and competing in the company of others is mutually beneficial.*

100

*All Goldens are capable of learning new skills.*

to track. It was an instant success, and we both derive great pleasure from it.

## Clicker Training

This is a simple but highly effective form of training, and dogs that are slow to respond to conventional forms of training frequently do very well at this. The clicker is a plastic, matchbox-sized object, with a metal insert that clicks when pressed. It isn't a loud noise, but dogs seem to hear it over a long distance and respond to it with interest. The idea is to 'click and treat' as the dog responds to commands. The Golden is very food-orientated, so this method of training suits him very well.

Training can be done on an individual basis, or as a part of one of the groups that exist throughout the country. I used it as a way of making a reluctant show dog be more attentive in the ring – I found I could 'click' quietly in my pocket to attract my dog without distracting others.

## The Kennel Club Good Citizen Dog Scheme

The scheme consists of three levels – bronze, silver and gold awards – as well as a Puppy Foundation Course, and each comprises practical tests for the dog alongside questions for the handler. The aim of all the levels is to promote responsible dog ownership.

### Puppy Foundation Assessment
Puppies who undertake this course will experience socialization and the rudiments essential for learning. Training through play and enjoyment is encouraged with the aim of teaching the puppy to respond to a handler who is aware of his needs. Puppies up to a year old are welcome to participate in the course, which must comprise of at least four weekly lessons. A puppy is expected to 'graduate' from the course before reaching a year old.

The puppy and handler are assessed throughout the course in a non-competitive environment, and both must pass all stages. As each exercise is covered, the assessor will rate the puppy as 'passed' or 'not ready'.

Clubs welcome puppies as soon as their vaccinations are complete, with the precise age being left to the discretion of the club. At the beginning of the course the handler will be given literature relating to, and covering every aspect of it. Owners will have group talks on the required topics, and further video and written material will be suggested.

*Components of the Course*
The owner will be taught to clean up after his dog in a responsible manner, and to ensure he wears a collar and tag, which would identify him in case of loss. Puppies should demonstrate that they know and respond to their names. They must also show that they play with their owners in a controlled manner, without play fighting.

Socialization is an important part of this course, and the puppy should show he is able to interact with other well behaved dogs without exhibiting aggression or fear. He should be

101

*Puppies should interact with humans and their siblings without aggression or fear.*

able to meet a stranger without being fearful, and should also be confident when hearing any of the sounds that he would encounter in everyday life.

Being able to handle one's dog is an important part of ensuring all is well, and the puppy should accept such an inspection of his body without fear or aggression.

A basic recall is required, and this will be tested in an enclosed space with someone holding the lead if required.

However briefly, the handler will need to demonstrate that the puppy will sit, stand and lie down. He must also demonstrate his willingness to walk on a lead, and also his ability to maintain a stay from any position, for at least ten seconds.

It is important that dogs relinquish objects they are holding when required to do so, and

this will be tested. Also, the puppy should accept a treat gently, and not snatch.

### The Bronze Award

When the course commences, owners will be given written information regarding the needs of a dog, signs of illness and responsible ownership. On the day of the test, owners will be required to give correct answers to three of the six questions relating to the written information.

The Bronze Award may be taken by all dogs, irrespective of age. They do not need to have taken the Puppy Foundation Assessment course. This is not a competitive course, but is intended towards well behaved dogs whose owners fully understand their needs, and who are mindful that their dogs must exist in the community and not annoy neighbours. Testing may be organized singly, or in groups.

Owners are taught the importance of cleaning up after their dogs, and must carry the means of doing so. They are made aware that it is illegal in this country for dogs to be without a collar and the means of identification; microchipping is not suffcient, and the dog must still wear a collar and tag with the owner's address. It is vital that the collar a dog wears is suited to its size, as many accidents are caused by frightened dogs jerking their heads out of a collar and escaping.

Owners will be tested on their ability to put on and remove a collar and lead safely.

The dog must demonstrate that it will walk on a lead without pulling or lagging back, and it must show controlled behaviour when going through a gate or door, and be calm while the gate or door is secured.

Walking amongst people and dogs is part of the test, which includes the dog remaining calm while the handler holds a conversation for one minute. The dog may adopt the sit, down or stand position during this conversation.

The dog must demonstrate he is capable of staying in any position for one minute. The position he is left in, must be the one adopted for the whole exercise. The dog is on the lead, which is dropped at the start of the exercise (it is not held to restrain him).

The dog should submit to thorough grooming, and any aggression or fear will be penalized. He must also permit the handler to inspect his body, including the mouth and teeth.

The recall while off the lead is part of this test, and the handler must be at least ten paces from the dog. This exercise should not promote the idea of dogs running loose in woods, parks and farmland.

### The Silver Award

The skills learned in the previous award should be added to, with an increase in complexity and a widening of experience. Like the previous award, the silver is not competitive. At the beginning of the course, handlers will be given literature relating to the exercises they will learn, the canine code, and responsibility and care, and at the end of the course they will be required to answer correctly six out of eight questions taken from the first two sections of the responsibility and care leaflet.

The dog will demonstrate controlled play at the instigation of the handler. No play fighting should be included.

Walking on a public highway is a part of everyday life nowadays, and the dog must be able to do this in a controlled manner. This exercise includes pausing at the kerb, crossing the road and continuing on the other side. Exposure to vehicles, prams, wheelchairs and people is part of the exercise.

Two different stay exercises are included: for the first the dog will be off the lead and remain steady until recalled by the handler from ten paces away. The second requires the dog to remain steady for two minutes, with

*Safe car travel is essential.*

the handler in sight. The handler will return to the dog.

Safe car travel is essential for dogs and their owners, and this part of the test will show that the dog is able to enter and leave a vehicle when commanded to do so. It will also show that the dog will remain quiet and controlled when the door is closed and the examiner and driver get into the car, and when the latter starts the engine.

The dog will be required to come away from an interesting group of people and dogs when called. For this exercise he will be off the lead, and should return without delay and have his lead secured.

Dogs that jump up on greeting are a menace, and the next exercise tests whether the dog will greet and be greeted without jumping up. Should he jump up he will still pass this section of the test as long as he gets down when instructed to do so. The owner and examiner should not unduly excite the dog.

Remaining indifferent while food is eaten or handled is the next part of the test, and probably the most taxing for the Golden Retriever! He will not pass if he begs or steals.

A stranger should examine the dog in a way that a vet might do so. Mild avoidance by the dog is permissible.

*The dog should come when called, even when distracted by people and dogs.*

## The Gold Award

The higher gold award tests the advanced training skills of dog and handler. The same literature will be given as before, and at the end of the programme, handlers should answer eight out of ten questions correctly from sections two and three of the responsibility and care leaflet.

Handler and dog should demonstrate advanced skills in road walking; these include being able to proceed at a fast and a slow pace across the road, then to continue the varied pace walking, and eventually to re-cross the road. Similar distractions to those encountered in the previous award should also be used at this level.

While walking free, the handler should be able to call the dog from at least ten paces away. Dog and handler are then required to continue walking, with the dog at the handler's walking side.

The next exercise is quite distinct from competitive heelwork. In this test, the dog should walk free beside the handler for at least forty paces. Both will change direction twice, and at one stage another dog and handler will walk past. The dog being tested will be off the lead at all times, until the lead is attached on completion of the exercise.

The dog will be required to stay in the down position for ten minutes, with the handler at least ten paces away. For half a minute, the handler should move out of sight.

For the next exercise, the dog's bed is provided in the form of either a blanket, a mat or an actual bed. From ten paces, the dog will be commanded to go to his bed.

Stopping on command could save a dog's life. For this exercise, the dog is stopped on command, at least ten paces from his handler. If the dog has been running, allowance is made for him to slow down.

Testing the dog to remain calmly tethered to a 2m line comes next. The owner will be out of sight for two to five minutes. An alternative test is to leave the dog in a room, where his reaction may be observed. The dog is not expected to be still for this exercise but must not bark, whine, howl, or be disruptive.

A test that is particularly diffcult for the Golden comes next: this is refusing food in the hand or bowl until told to eat. There should be a 3–5sec pause between the presentation of the food and the command to eat.

Examination of the dog by a stranger is also tested. The dog will be on a lead throughout while his whole body is examined.

All the above awards and the puppy programme are great fun to do, and it is diffcult to decide who derives the most fun from the exercises, the dogs or the handlers. One thing is certain, that on completion of one or more of the courses, the owner will have a far better understanding of his dog's needs, and the dog will be much better to live with. Such a scheme was long overdue here, and now that we have it, it is hoped that many more people each year will take advantage of it.

## Flyball

This is one of the newer activities for dogs and is tremendously exciting for both the participants and the spectators. Many clubs exist throughout Britain for the promotion of this activity. Essentially a team sport, the number of dogs in each team is at the discretion of the organizer. No switching of dogs from team to team is permitted once the runners have been declared.

The course consists of four hurdles, over which each dog jumps, then it triggers the box to release the ball, which it carries to the handler. As soon as each dog crosses the finishing line, the next is sent to perform the same moves. The first team to have its final dog cross the finishing line is declared the winner, and the team providing the best of three runs goes on to the next heat.

The hurdles used are the same height for all dogs, 30.9cm (12in), and are 61cm (24in) wide. The trap is either sprung or padded.

Teams supply their own boxes, which eject a tennis ball as the dog depresses a bar.

To be a spectator at flyball is exciting, with the atmosphere closely resembling greyhound racing. The noise level is deafening, and not all of it comes from the dogs!

## Gundog Activities

All breeds of gundog were initially bred to work, and most, given the chance, will show some natural aptitude. In some dogs this will need to be encouraged more than in others, but there are very few that will not willingly participate in at least one discipline, be it retrieving, searching or marking. Few pet dogs will automatically manage these activities, but if they show an interest in, or have a talent for, at least one exercise, then there is a good foundation on which to work.

Initially it was only possible to work a dog if you had connections with an organized

*Flyball is exciting for spectators and participants.*

*Dummies are used to test the dog's working ability.*

shoot on various estates throughout the country, but now the majority of gundog clubs offer this facility. Just how far you wish to go into the world of competitive gundog work is a matter of personal choice, but the options are very wide indeed.

Whichever section of working you decide to become involved in, your dog will need some basic obedience first. It is common sense that if you can't trust a dog off the lead for fear of it bolting, it would not be an ideal candidate with which to start the more advanced work of retrieving.

### Show Gundog Working Certificate

The Show Gundog Working Certificate qualification is needed for gundogs that gain their Show Champion title (by winning three challenge certificates under three different judges), to enable them to hold the much coveted title of Champion. The aim of such a qualification is to show that not only does the dog fulfil the criteria of the Kennel Club breed standard in conformation and movement, but it is also able to perform the basic exercises required of its specific breed.

It is expected that the dogs who participate will be under the control of their handlers while off the lead. They should not be gun-shy, and should retrieve from water as well as from land; it is also essential that they are already acquainted with freshly shot game, and that they will retrieve it.

Owners who wish their dogs to participate in exercises leading to the Show Gundog Working Certificate may enter them at a show gundog working day, or have them tested at a field trial meeting (separately from competing in the trial itself, which is for very advanced dogs). Dogs entering a show gundog working day will be required to have already won at least one first prize in the show ring, at a championship show.

The day will start with the dogs being tested in line. This usually involves each dog being flanked by two guns, so it is essential to accustom your dog to gunfire at a distance, gradually moving him closer to the sound, before you subject him to such a test. While the guns do not stand next to the dogs, they are not too far away – at my last test the guns on each side were approximately 20ft

*The dogs and handlers stand in numerical order.*

(6m) away. Even at that distance, the retort of the gun is very loud, especially when you consider the great sensitivity of the dog's hearing. Many dogs that were good initially have been ruined by being shot over at too close range.

The dogs are off the lead (usually one at a time), sitting at heel when the guns are fired. There must be no barking or whining, and it goes without saying that any dog exhibiting a fear of gunfire (as opposed to surprise) would fail the test.

One of my dogs would hide inside the skirt of my long waxed coat if it was snowing or raining; he would then look out of the vent at the back, making the other handlers convulse laughing. He was quite steady to shot, but loathed inclement weather. On the day of the Show Gundog Working Certificate it snowed heavily, and Percy retreated to his waxed shelter. The judge said 'Is that dog shy, madam?' and I replied that he certainly was not, but merely hated getting wet. The judge retreated, muttering 'It's supposed to be a working gundog!' – but we gained our certificate!

Dogs will need to show that they are not gun-shy, and are reasonably steady. A dog that on one or two occasions ran in to retrieve before being sent to do so would not necessarily fail the test, but one that habitually ran in throughout the day would be unlikely to pass. Whining or barking is just about the worst thing your dog could do on the day (the very worst being eating the game!).

Dogs are required to hunt for a bird, which is often one that has been placed in cover. They should not be put off by brambles or dense vegetation, and should retrieve the bird tenderly to hand, without mouthing or crushing. Judges will examine the bird to check that it shows no signs of puncture marks or crushed ribs.

Dogs must show that they will retrieve from water. As it is impossible to predict

*Willingness to retrieve from water is a characteristic of the breed.*

where birds will fall, if a natural retrieve of game from water is not possible, a dummy may be substituted. If a water test is impossible at the time when the above exercises take place, then it may be staged at a different location, on a different day.

If your dog fulfils the criteria for this award, you will be awarded the certificate at the end of the day, which will be signed by the judges and the secretary of the society organizing the test.

This award is much coveted by owners and not only permits the dog to hold the full title of Champion, but also secures entry in the Kennel Club Stud Book.

## Gundog Working Tests

Gundog working tests give dogs and handlers the opportunity to work through an artificially created shooting day, without any game being shot. These tests are organized by registered societies.

Dogs entering the gundog working test will have attained a higher standard than is needed for the Show Gundog Working Certificate. They should not run in when the guns are fired, nor when the dummy falls.

*Speed is required when retrieving.*

*Credit is given for the dog's ability to use his nose and mark the fall.*

Ideally, a simulated drive should take place, with the dogs free. They should also be tested in water. The dog is expected to mark the fall accurately, and speed is required for the retrieve and pick-up.

The handler should work his dog in a quiet, controlled manner, and credit will be given to dogs showing natural ability in performing the set tasks. If the dog changes the retrieve article this is considered a serious fault, as is whining and barking. Running in or chasing, failing to enter water, and generally uncontrolled behaviour will also be penalized.

## Field Trials

Golden Retrievers from working breeding are generally the choice of owners who wish to aspire to field trials, which constitute the highest level of competitive gundog work. The dogs are more lightly built than the show type, and are almost exclusively darker in colour.

Few dogs may be trained up to field trial standard in under two years. Much skill is needed on the part of the handler-trainer, and only those whose dogs have been trained to the highest level should consider entering a trial.

*This agile dog makes light of jumping a hedge.*

A whole book in itself would be needed to cover the training and requirements of entering a trial. Those who are interested may obtain further details from fieldtrials@the-kennel-club.org.uk

## Agility Classes

Unbelievably, this activity is approaching its thirtieth year. The public's first glimpse of this most entertaining competition was at Crufts. Entry is open to all Kennel Club registered dogs. They do not have to be pure bred, as entry in the Activity Register qualifies them for competition.

It should be stressed that agility tests are for *fit* humans and dogs: they are very fast, and it would be unthinkable to subject any but the fittest dogs to this form of competition.

There are 300 licensed agility tests held each year, so there is plenty of opportunity to compete. Most people are familiar with the events held at Crufts and the international Horse of the Year Show, through wide television coverage. Although the Border Collie is the dog perfectly suited to agility, Golden Retrievers compete well — though these are frequently the working type, of lighter build.

As it is a competition run against the clock, the heavier type of Golden Retriever just would not have the requisite speed.

The obstacles used demonstrate the dog's ability to jump, weave, crawl and balance, as well as to run at speed. Not only is the dog's ability being tested, but also the handler's skill in training and direction.

Even if the speed and range of an 'offcial' course is too taxing for many dogs, there is nothing to stop any owner constructing a modified course, and simply having fun. Most handymen could construct the set of poles needed for the 'weave', as well as low hurdles and a see-saw. Dogs love the tunnel exercise, and once they have learned it, they just want to do it again and again. Tunnels are available from many firms that make playground toys for toddlers, and if you want the real thing, there are now companies that manufacture all the equipment needed for agility tests. Try it! It is such fun for dogs and handlers.

## Dancing with Dogs

The offcial title for this is 'Heelwork to Music', and you have only to watch this newest of activities for dogs to realize just

*The enjoyment of dogs and handlers is evident.*

how much the participants enjoy it. Training is based on motivation and reward, and points are given for the variety of moves included, for how well each move is executed, and how smoothly one leads into another. Points are also given for how well the music and the moves match. Moves performed by the dog include twirls, back to back with the handler, and the bow.

This activity is not for the novice, because much skill is needed to train dogs in this way. Those who have the most success are almost exclusively the handlers who excel in competitive obedience.

## Obedience

This topic is vast, and it would need a whole book all to itself to cover it adequately. From the moment you train your puppy to sit, you are both participating in obedience; the level you wish to reach is up to the individual.

Competition ranges from the simple tests at the local pet show right through to the Obedience Championships at Crufts. There are, of course, many possibilities in between.

Whatever level you choose, you will need to train your dog in the company of others, so joining a club is essential. Tests range from beginners right up to Class C, from where obedience champions emerge. This is a much coveted title, and the few Golden Retrievers who have held it have made others in the breed feel very proud.

Exercises at all levels are based on heelwork, sitting, the down, and staying with the handler both in and out of sight, and the retrieve. The more advanced tests require the dog to be sent away, to a marked area. The dog also needs to perform scent discrimination, where he finds and retrieves a specific article from a selection of identical articles. Arguably the most diffcult exercise is distance control, where the dog must sit, stand, and lie down across the ring from his handler, without stepping outside the designated area.

Such exercises are for real training addicts, but there is nothing to stop you doing as much or as little as you both enjoy.

*Whichever level you choose, training in the company of others is essential.*

## The Southern Golden Retriever Society Display Team

*Friends formed the now famous Southern Golden Retriever Society's display team.*

Seven years ago, eight friends who really enjoyed training and having fun with their dogs, got together to form the Southern Golden Retriever Society Display Team. They had already gained their Kennel Club Good Citizens Gold Award at the society's training club at Wrotham, in Kent.

The eight grew to twelve, and now the team consists of sixteen dogs and handlers with four reserves. They perform obedience to music, and have probably done more than anyone to promote the Golden Retriever in a favourable light. They are keen to stress that their dogs are not competitive obedience participants, but are essentially family pets. The enjoyment of dogs, handlers and audience is quite wonderful to observe.

Originally they performed at fêtes throughout the South East, and their first big event was a display at their own club's Championship Show. They were then invited to appear at the Kennel Club's 'Discover Dogs', at Earls Court in 2003. This most successful performance led to their appearance at Crufts. This has now become an annual event, and is a great favourite with the crowds. Other high-profile appearances have included the Kent County Show, the two-day Paws in the Park Show, the Wag and Bone Show, and at Birmingham Championship Show.

The team has also appeared on *Blue Peter*, and all the dogs were awarded the coveted Blue Peter badge! The team returned to the *Blue Peter* studios to film footage for a nationwide competition.

The team has twice appeared on the live BBC Crufts coverage, and some of the dogs formed a guard of honour in 2007 as Ben Fogle and Clare Balding entered the studio. The programme ended with the presenters being surrounded by a sea of Golden Retrievers who then gave an excerpt from their routine.

This just goes to show what may be achieved by ordinary dog owners who enjoy their pets,

*The annual display at Crufts receives rapturous applause.*

## The Southern Golden Retriever Society Display Team *(continued)*

*The team in the* Blue Peter *garden.*

*Such displays show these dogs as obedient family pets.*

and who are capable of bringing enjoyment to others. Children love these displays, and at the end of the routine are invited into the ring to meet the dogs. There could be no better publicity for this lovely breed, showing them as obedient family pets who love everyone. Their press offcer, Jan Cook, wrote:

The team enjoys showing the public the joy of owning well behaved dogs, and the dogs love it. Golden Retrievers seem particularly suited to what the team does, as they are a very sociable breed and think they belong to a doggy youth club.

What better publicity could this breed have?

## Mind Games

You don't have to participate in any of these formal competitions to enjoy your dog; there are many simple things you can both enjoy, without going to organized classes.

### Seek

The Golden has a good nose, and any exercise where he has to find something will further this natural ability. Start this game over a distance of just a few paces, with the dog walking to heel. Drop the article (food is good at this stage), and continue walking. Stop, about turn so the dog is facing the dropped object, and command 'Seek!'. Then head him in the direction of the article, and usually its scent will do the rest. Expand this exercise by hiding items in long grass.

When your dog obviously has the idea of what you expect of him, progress to sending him to find items you have hidden outside the day before. Such games can be played indoors in inclement weather.

### Tracking

It is not just the scent of the article dragged to make a track, but the scent of the grass it bruises in passing. Start by dragging something (a sock with an orange inside is ideal) over a short distance, and encourage your dog when he obviously follows the path of the dragged object. A favourite toy can be used, and the more proficient the dog becomes, the lighter the drag object should be. Very little bruising will result from a very light object passing over grass, so more skill is required on the dog's part. Hide a treat at the very end of the track.

## Catch
Goldens adore chasing and catching anything, and flat discs are a firm favourite. I have never had a dog that didn't enjoy the game. Make sure you never throw the disc at the dog: it should be thrown as hard as possible, *away* from the dog. One slight drawback of this game is that the dogs sometimes use the disc as a chew article, first retrieving it, and then dashing off to a quiet corner to have a nibble! These discs are definitely not chew-proof!

## Bubbles
My latest acquisition is a battery-operated bubble gun. When the trigger is depressed, bubbles are released from the canister of liquid screwed on to the bottom. This works best on a breezy day when the bubbles travel good distances. As these bubbles have various meat and poultry aromas, they are very attractive to dogs; my youngsters jump and snap to burst them, but the old dogs enjoy bursting the bubbles that come to rest on the ground, and then lick the grass where they

*Swimming is the best form of exercise.*

have burst. I have never had anything else give so much enjoyment to the dogs.

## Water Games

### Swimming
This is the best exercise your dog can ever have, as he is weightless in water. So many hydrotherapy pools now exist that there is bound to be one within easy reach, and some of these pools allow owners to swim with their dogs. There are also still beaches in the UK where dogs are welcome, so swimming at these is possible. Remember, your dog will need rinsing with clear water after being in the salty sea water.

*Bubble machines provide much enjoyment.*

## Paddling Pools

Golden Retrievers adore water, and the pleasure derived from watching them splash about makes the effort of building a pool worthwhile. If you decide to construct one along the lines of a pond, take care with your choice of liner, as sharp claws soon tear plastic sheeting.

However you decide to make your pool, ensure it has a means of drainage (and somewhere to drain into), as the water quickly becomes very muddy. The best dog pool I have seen was a very large child's paddling pool, made from a more pliable type of plastic than is used for buckets and bowls. The 'give' in the fabric rendered it robust enough not to split, and the thickness prevented dogs' nails puncturing the surface.

Unless you cover your pool, you will have a strange assortment of occupants each morning, ranging from frogs and toads to hedgehogs. The former are fine, but the latter will drown unless there is an escape ramp. It is perhaps easier to drain the pool each night.

## In Conclusion

Finally, it really does not matter what you do with your Golden, as long as you do something, and the more activities you do together, the greater the bond between you. Goldens are such fun dogs that they deserve to participate in some of these activities. To have such a dog, and all it does is just go for a walk then lie by the fire, does that dog a great disservice. It also denies the owner a great deal of pleasure.

*Goldens love anything to do with water.*

*On hot days, dogs will sit in water troughs to cool down.*

*Participation in most things is possible!*

# 8 Health Problems

The healthy dog is a joy to see, with his glossy coat, bright eyes and well toned body; but sometimes, however well we feed and care for our dogs, things go wrong. The first sign that all is not well is a change in the dog's behaviour: where formerly he has been full of energy, he is now lethargic and dull; and often a lack of appetite, particularly in a dog that usually eats with great enthusiasm, is an indication that all is not well.

Any discharge from the eyes or ears, or indeed from any other orifice, should be investigated. A dog's smell is a reliable guide, because we are all familiar with how our dogs smell, and any deviation from the norm should be viewed with suspicion.

Strange lumps and bumps appearing anywhere on the body need investigating. Often they will be harmless, fatty lumps, but an expert is needed to differentiate

*A healthy dog is a joy to see*

*Many lumps are harmless, but all should be investigated.*

between the harmless bump and the malignant growth.

A health check should be done while grooming. The comb will often alert the groomer to a new lump or crusty area, though fingers are your best guide, and the dog owner should become accustomed to running his hands through the dog's coat as he grooms. Ensure that 'hidden' areas are not forgotten, such as between the toes and behind the ears; also much could lurk in the dense feathering in the dog's hindquarters, so part this and examine with care. The same should be done with the tail, where the feathering could mask problems.

The Golden Retriever, in common with many other breeds, is prone to inherited conditions. Schemes exist to control and reduce the incidence of such problems: for example, we have schemes for x-raying and scoring hips and elbows, and for testing eyes; and although there is no offcial scheme for heart testing in the UK, some breeders routinely have cardiac tests for their dogs. The ideal is that only dogs with acceptable scores for hips and elbows, and with eyes clear of inherited defects, should be bred from.

Unfortunately, there is nothing to stop unscrupulous breeders producing litters from dysplastic, sight-impaired dogs and bitches. The onus is always on the buyer to ask to see all certificates of clearance for both parents before buying a puppy: it is a case of *caveat emptor* ('buyer beware'). Fortunately there are also many caring, responsible breeders who take full advantage of all the health schemes, and who only breed from sound, healthy stock. Such breeders will be proud to show the prospective puppy buyer the certificates proving their dogs are free from inherited defects.

## The Eyes

Eyes should be bright and free of discharge. Temporary irritation may occur after a car journey, where the dog has been permitted to look out of an open window, however eye drops should remedy this problem within two days.

Foreign bodies will cause the eye to become inflamed. Most deposits will float away with the increased tear production, but if the condition persists on the second day, veterinary intervention is indicated.

Occasionally tear ducts will become blocked, and the fur below the inner corner of the eye will be tear-stained. These ducts will need to be examined by a vet, and this is generally done by the introduction of a bright liquid that will visibly flow down the nose if the ducts are clear. If they remain blocked, surgical intervention will be required.

### The Eye Scheme

The scheme whereby we may have our dogs' eyes tested has been in existence for over forty years. The first eye-testing session was held in conjunction with the Golden Retriever Club's Championship Show in 1966, with Dr Keith Barnett offciating, and it was a great shock to those present when almost a quarter of the dogs tested that day failed. In retrospect it is surprising that so many passed, because before that day we had no way of assessing the eye status of our dogs, and many affected dogs and bitches would have been inadvertently mated together.

Many older breeders were suspicious of the scheme, while the newer breeders wondered what they had become involved in; but eventually most gained confidence in it, and took full advantage of what was offered.

Now, the British Veterinary Association together with the Kennel Club and the International Sheep Dog Society offer eye testing so that breeders and owners may tell whether or not their dogs are affected by inherited eye defects. In the light of the knowledge gained from these tests, breeders can reduce or eliminate these problems being inherited by the puppies they produce.

Goldens are usually eye tested around their first birthday, but schemes are available for testing whole litters (known as 'litter screening'), as young as six to twelve weeks.

### The Eye Test

The BVA selects a panel of eye specialists, situated throughout Britain, who are qualified to test eyes and issue certificates. The various Golden Retriever Clubs organize testing days, and the service is offered at a reduced fee. You do not need a veterinary reference to have your dog's eyes tested, but simply need to make an appointment yourself. You must present your dog's registration certificate at the start of the test, and if applicable his micro-chip or tattoo will be checked.

No sedation or anaesthetic is required for the test itself, but the dog will have eye drops administered thirty minutes before the test. These do not harm him, but he will display an increased sensitivity to light for several hours afterwards.

*Eye examination using an ophthalmoscope.*

*Stuart Ellis examines a dog, using a slit lamp.*

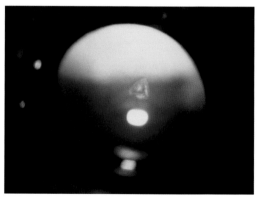

*Inherited posterior polar cataract.*

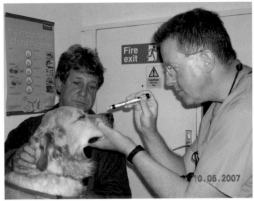

*Pen-torch examination.*

*Non-inherited cataract.*

He will be placed on a table in a darkened room, and the panellist will examine his eyes with an ophthalmoscope and other lenses. The whole procedure will take five minutes, and you will be issued with a certificate stating whether your dog is 'clear' or 'affected'.

Each eye is tested separately, and a failure for one condition does not automatically constitute a failure for the others. However, it must be made clear that a failure in *any* of the conditions makes the dog unsuitable for

*Indirect ophthalmoscopy examination.*

breeding for fear of passing the problem to future generations.

Eyes should be tested annually, and at each test all the previous certificates should be shown. When the owner signs the eye-test form, he automatically agrees that data may be used in research programmes, and that the results of the test may be published. These results appear in the Kennel Club's *Breed Record Supplement*, published quarterly; as the failures and passes are published, it is not possible to conceal your dog's eye status.

**Eye Conditions**

*Cataract*

Cataract refers to any opacity of the lens, and both eyes may be affected (bilateral), or only one (unilateral). Puppies may be born with cataract, or it may have a later onset, but to be classed as hereditary, the position of the cataract is vital. Those that are small and non-progressive will have no effect on vision, whereas the progressive type, which is less common, grows until the whole lens is affected.

Cataract should not be confused with the clouding of the eyes seen in old dogs: this is nuclear sclerosis, which is quite different and not inherited.

*Progressive Retinal Atrophy (PRA)*

PRA is a condition where the light-sensitive part of the retina is gradually destroyed, and blindness results. The Golden Retriever is prone to central progressive retinal atrophy (CPRA), where spots of pigment appear on the retina; the density gradually increases, compromising the sight.

Even severely affected dogs are able to detect moving objects, but static forms confuse them. Often the first sign of a dog being affected is when, having been called, he approaches in an arc, rather than a straight line, even walking right past his owner. It is common for the dog to return to a gate post or a tree, when he is obviously confusing its upright form with that of a human.

*Multifocal Retinal Dysplasia (MRD)*

MRD occurs when the retina fails to develop properly; an ophthalmoscope will detect folds in it. Much controversy arose in the Golden Retriever world when this condition was added to the list of certifiable defects. The main concern of breeders was that the more unscrupulous would delay having their dogs' eyes tested because minor folds were known to grow out, and would disappear altogether. Consequently these dogs would gain certificates of clearance

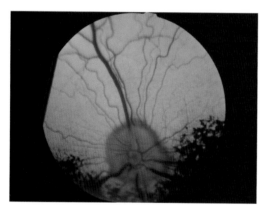

*Normal retina.*

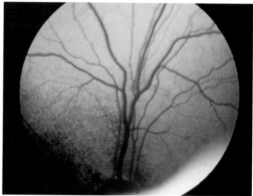

*Multi-focal retinal dysplasia with y-shaped lesion.*

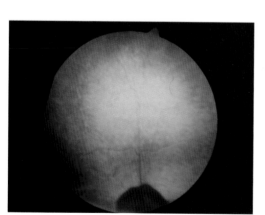

*Advanced CPRA and blind.*

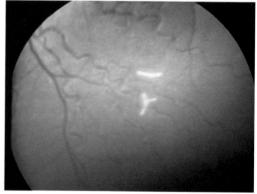

*Multi-focal retinal dysplasia in a puppy.*

from MRD, when in fact they were clinically affected.

Another cause for concern was that the adult stud dogs and brood bitches of the day, by virtue of being adult, were at a stage where slight folds would already have grown out, so it would never be known if these dogs were affected or not.

The arguments still rage, and lectures and papers on the subject have done little to calm the anger and quell the suspicions of some breeders. Most feel that they should have been involved when the condition was under review, rather than having the test presented as a *fait accompli*.

*Entropion*

Entropion is an eye condition for which there is no testing scheme; nevertheless, affected animals should not be bred from. Symptoms are clearly visible to the owner, as one or both eyelids turn inwards, causing the lashes to scrub against the eye. Tears will stain the fur as they run down the muzzle. Affected dogs rub their eyes, so exacerbating the problem. It is an acutely painful condition, which can only be cured by surgery.

*Ectropion*

Ectropion occurs when the eyelid turns outwards, and is less commonly seen in the

*Horner's Syndrome, shown with the characteristic drooping lower lid.*

Golden than entropion. Again, affected animals should not be used for breeding.

*Horner's Syndrome*

Horner's syndrome is not an inherited condition, but when present it seems to cause more distress to the owner than to the dog, because of the dog's altered facial expression. The first sign of this problem is a droopy lower lid, making the animal look like a bloodhound in appearance.

This condition is frequently the result of a trauma, and in the days of the barbaric choke chain was linked to its harsh use. Ear infections that inflame the surrounding tissue may be a cause. A brain tumour may lead to this condition, though this is rare.

Phenylephrine eye drops reverse the condition temporarily to enable the damage to be examined. If the pupils dilate it is likely that the cause of the problem is in the middle ear, or is idiopathic. If the pupil does not dilate, then the lesion is likely to be in the brain, neck or chest. In most dogs, the condition will right itself in three or four months. Artificial tears will need to be used during this time to stop the conjunctiva drying out.

# Hip Dysplasia

For many years the Golden was singled out as the breed that suffered most significantly from hip dysplasia, although many more were affected to a lesser degree. However, after years of careful breeding and better nutrition, great improvements have been made, and many dogs now have the desired low scores.

HD is when the hip joint develops abnormally; this development is influenced by hereditary and non-hereditary factors, so is said to be multi-factorial. The hip joint is a ball-and-socket assembly, and each or both parts may be affected. The abnormality may be slight or severe, though even severely affected joints may be disguised by relatively sound movement. Breeders who maintain that they know their dogs are sound because they move well, and therefore have no need of scoring, are talking nonsense, because the only way to know whether dogs are affected or not, and how severely, is to have an x-ray, which is then scored.

Dogs are x-rayed for hip dysplasia after they are one year old, because before this the growth plates will not have closed.

## The X-Ray

The dog will be either sedated or anaesthetized, and then placed on his back in a plastic cradle, which supports him in the required position. His forelegs will be stretched forwards, and at the same time the hind legs will be stretched and rotated, and an x-ray taken; this will be developed within minutes. Most vets will voice an opinion as to whether the plates show hips that will score above or below the breed average.

When presenting a dog for this x-ray, the Kennel Club registration certificate must be produced. The owner is required to fill in a form stating the dog's details, including the first three generations of his pedigree (remember to take a copy with you, unless you have an exceptionally good memory). Once you sign the form, you agree to the resulting data being used in future studies, and the score published. Micro-chipped dogs will have their chips read.

The x-ray plates are then sent away to be scored by a panel of experts, and it usually takes at least a month for the results to be sent to your vet. Bitches that are in season should not be x-rayed, because a less good score will be achieved at this time; for bitches, the optimum time for x-raying is half way between seasons.

## The Scoring Process

Each hip is scored independently, with nine areas being assessed (*see* below). The photograph of the perfect hip with a 0:0 score illustrates some of these features. The other photographs show obvious changes between an ideal hip and an affected one. What is impossible to show is the marked difference in the way that affected animals deal with HD; therefore it is possible for a dog that is only slightly affected to be lamer than one that is severely dysplastic. Muscle, exercise, nutrition and management all play a part in how individual animals cope with the problem.

The following areas are the nine that are assessed:

**Norberg angle** This measurement shows the degree of dislocation, and should be at least 105 degrees: the greater the dislocation, the less the angle.

**Subluxation** The fit of a joint: in the hip it shows how the ball (femoral head) is separated from the socket, the acetabulum – the poorer the fit, the greater the degree of HD.

**Cranial acetabular edge** The upper curve of the socket: HD is characterized by a flattening of this edge.

**Dorsal acetabular edge** In HD, this rim of the socket will show extra bone formation. It is the degree of this formation that is assessed.

**Cranial effective acetabular rim** Where the two former scored areas meet in a point: the more rounded this area is, the more extra bone growth would occur, with the later development of arthritis. It is obvious that the less smooth these areas are, the greater will be the degree of resulting pain.

**Acetabular fossa** The ligament attaching the ball to the socket: the presence of HD marked by new growth makes this area difcult to see clearly.

**Caudal acetabular edge** New bone formation is present in HD at this site, which is the opposite equivalent to the cranial effective acetabular rim.

**Femoral head/neck extosis** This ball-shaped joint will show new bone growth in the presence of HD, so preventing its neat fit into the socket. The neck of the joint will have an altered, thickened shape.

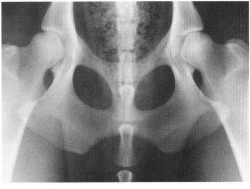

*X-ray showing an 8:10 hip score, which is just below breed average.*

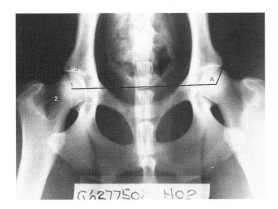

*X-ray showing 0:0 hip score.*
*A=Norberg angle; 1=femoral head; 2=femoral neck;*
*3=cranial acetabular edge; 4=cranial effective*
*acetabular rim; 5=caudal acetabular edge.*

**Femoral head recontouring** The slackened joint resulting from HD will lead to an altered shaping of the ball (femoral head).

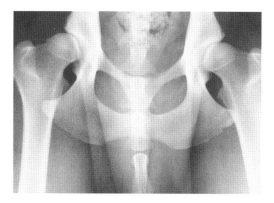

*The poor fit of the femoral head into the socket of this 30:30 score is obvious.*

The hip-scoring scheme only presents an accurate picture if owners submit the x-rays of every dog taken. It is very tempting not to send in for scoring the x-ray plates that show poor hips, fearing the results will reflect badly on your kennel. But if all the bad were withheld and only the good submitted, then a false average would result and the resulting data would give inaccurate information to breeders. The average, in any case, is false, as the number it gives does not take into account the many thousands of Golden Retrievers that are never x-rayed and scored.

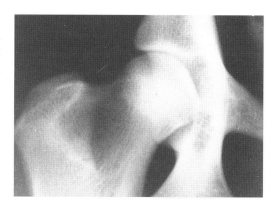

*In this close-up view of one hip from the 0:0 hip score, the excellent fit is obvious.*

The perfect hip will gain a 0:0 score, which represents no problem with the right and left hip. The most severely dysplastic hips would gain the maximum combined score of 106. Each of the parts of the hip described above is scored out of five, except the caudal acetabular edge, which is scored out of six.

At the present time, the average score for the breed is a total of nineteen (be aware that this does not represent nineteen for each hip). We should strive only to breed from animals having this, or a lower score. It must always be borne in mind that hips are just one part of the dog, albeit an important part, but the whole animal must be considered when breeding.

Dr Malcolm Willis is the geneticist who collects the data from all x-rayed dogs (not just Golden Retrievers), and produces his findings in a published form at regular intervals. Such results are invaluable, and the serious breeder would not proceed without referring to this information. It shows the results when animals of certain lines are mated together, and helps breeders avoid the pitfalls of mating together lines that are seen to produce higher scores. No scheme is perfect, but this is the best we have, and many of us are immensely grateful to Dr Willis for enabling us to have this information.

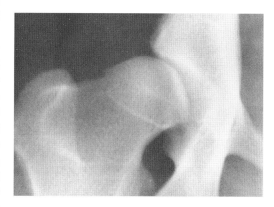

*In this close-up view of one hip from the dog with the 30:30 score, the difference in shape of the femoral head and degree of fit into the acetabular socket is obvious.*

The only way ahead is to x-ray and score as many dogs as possible, being guided by the results, but never losing sight of the whole dog. Thus the most perfect hips and clear eyes can never be a substitute for poor temperament.

# General Problems

To cover all the diseases and ailments specific to the dog would require volumes, and not just the space of one chapter. Those covered here provide relevant information for the pet owner and the serious breeder, both of whom wish to detect changes in the condition of their animals. While it is easy to spot dogs that are off colour, generally it is more diffcult to know *why*.

### Problems in the Ears
The insides of the ears should be pink and clean, without any offensive (yeasty) smell. It is normal for dogs to produce ear wax, which is much darker than the human variety. Some dogs will produce more than others, without any underlying cause. Resist the urge to poke about in the ear, as a sudden jerk of the head could result in damage. Clean only the outer parts of the ear, which may be wiped with the moistened cloths used for babies. Squeeze these wipes before use to remove excess moisture. Products are available for dissolving wax, which will come to the surface, where it may be wiped away.

Excessive ear shaking or scratching requires veterinary attention, as foreign bodies could be present. Grass seeds are the most likely suspects, and these do much damage if not professionally removed. Ear mites are another cause of irritation, particularly if you have a cat, from where they could transmit to your dog.

The flap of the ear (or pinna) should be examined for lumps or crinkles. Excessive shaking of the head (as may be caused by mites) can cause a haematoma, where the flap can fill with blood. The size of this bag-like swelling is alarming, but treatment is effective and simple. The blood will be drained and a steroid injected. The condition would resolve itself over a number of weeks if left untreated, but the flap would remain permanently convoluted.

If drainage is not effective, then the vet will resort to surgery because this prevents the pinna becoming deformed and scarred. The operation involves suturing the layers of the ear together to prevent fluid reforming.

### Problems with the Nails
Nails may be colourless or black. If allowed to grow over-long they will split, exposing the quick, and become infected, causing much pain. Some dogs naturally grow longer nails, and it is a fallacy to believe exercise will keep them short: long nails must be clipped regularly, or severe discomfort will be caused to the dog.

Dew claws can grow full circle, with the point entering the flesh, causing abscesses and severe pain. This is commonly seen in old dogs, and is the result of neglect. Regular inspection is vital.

The nail bed may become infected (*paronchyia*) when a fragment of grass enters between the nail and the skin. This infection is persistent, sometimes resisting antibiotics, and the nail may need to be removed so that treatment is effective.

When regularly checking nails, it is important to feel deep into the 'webbing' between the toes. In wet weather the fur will matt into hard lumps, which is the canine equivalent of our walking with a stone in our shoe. These matts must be removed with blunt-ended scissors.

### Lameness
Lameness that occurs without being the result of obvious trauma is diffcult to diagnose. Many owners are familiar with the dog

that persistently limps and which they have x-rayed, only to find that no obvious cause can be detected. Usually, after a period of rest and a course of anti-inflammatory tablets, the condition rights itself.

Persistent lameness needs further investigation to rule out more sinister causes, such as bone tumours. Most bone tumours are osteosarcomas, highly malignant tumours that affect the long bones of the legs. Swelling is obvious when the condition is advanced, but is not seen in the early stages. This condition affects the large and giant breeds, so Goldens are not exempt.

The prognosis is poor, because although amputation is possible, the tumour spreads rapidly to other sites, usually the lungs. Once the secondary tumours have developed, survival time is unlikely beyond six months.

### Lumps and Bumps

These are most frequently discovered during a grooming session. Unless you are positive as to the cause of the swelling, veterinary investigation is essential.

### Swollen Lymph Glands

Swollen glands most commonly occur in response to infection. Glands will also swell for more serious reasons, such as the presence of cancer, so it is essential that any such abnormality is investigated.

### Tumours

This is a blanket word for any swelling. Another word for tumours is neoplasm, which means the cells are rapidly growing and dividing. Some tumours are harmless (benign) and do no harm to the dog, although some become so large that they need to be removed to make the animal more comfortable, or on aesthetic grounds.

The tumours that need rapid removal are the malignant type, which spread to other organs. Lymphomas and lymphosarcomas may respond to chemotherapy. Generally speaking, carcinomas and sarcomas are not as responsive. Mammary tumours are treatable with surgery, as are melanomas and other skin tumours.

### Lipoma

A lipoma is an unsightly swelling, frequently seen in older bitches. These are fatty tumours for which surgical removal is successful. It is not essential to remove them unless they cause problems for the dog; for instance, some grow so large that movement is compromised, or the dog is unable to lie down comfortably.

### Mammary Tumours

These are lumps felt in the mammary glands. Almost half of these are mammary adenocarcinomas, which may be surgically removed; however, by the time this is done, they may have formed 'secondary' tumours elsewhere.

### Warts

Any small skin lump with a stalk may be described as a wart. Older dogs frequently have warts on the muzzle, eyelids and head. Unless they become large and cause discomfort most owners ignore them, but any skin growth should be viewed with suspicion and investigated.

Warts may be frozen to remove them, a process called cryosurgery. Skin tumours that are malignant must be removed, and the veterinary surgeon will advise as to further treatment.

### Problems in the Mouth

Any unusual odour from the mouth should be investigated. Usually it will be nothing more than the result of something unpleasant eaten by the dog (a common Golden Retriever habit!), but occasionally it is a warning that attention is required. Mouth tumours could be the cause.

Periodontal disease is common with older dogs, and may be seen as inflammation and swelling where the teeth and gums meet. The teeth will need cleaning to remove the deposits (calculus) that have formed. Antibiotics will be required to combat infection, and future brushing is essential. Hard biscuits will help prevent the build-up of calculus, as will the safe calcium bones (the white chalky ones that don't shatter).

Goldens are notorious for getting things, usually sticks, stuck across the roof of their mouth. Although sticks must never be thrown for dogs because of the possible injury that may occur, this breed cannot resist those found on walks. When these become wedged, the dog will paw frantically at his mouth, salivating copiously. A sharp tug downwards is needed to dislodge the offending item.

Other objects that become lodged are not so instantly obvious. A dog came into Rescue and appeared to have diffculty closing his mouth. He was salivating copiously, and I instantly suspected a deformed jaw or mouth tumour; the smell from his mouth was extremely putrid. Investigation revealed a bottle cap wedged over a back tooth, and from the degree of inflammation and the quantity of detritus that had collected, it seemed the cap had been in place for a considerable time. Unbelievably, his owner hadn't noticed!

**Problems with the Skin**

The dog's skin should be loose, as if it were a size too large for his frame. Tight skin is a sign of dehydration, and when lifted up will stay as a ridge, known as 'tenting'.

Scratching and thereby causing the skin to become inflamed is a common occurrence, but all dogs scratch for a reason. Broken hair will reveal if a dog is biting itself. Hair loss once or twice a year is normal, as dogs

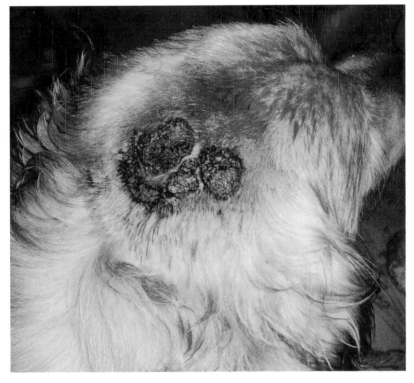

*Eczema is a common Golden Retriever problem.*

need to moult; the coat will come out over a period of weeks, and as the old fur comes away, so the new, healthy coat will be growing. Any deviation from this cycle of moulting and then re-growth should be investigated by the vet.

Bare patches on the skin need instant treatment. If the hair is lost on both sides of the body in a symmetrical pattern, the cause is likely to be hormonal.

Circular bare patches are almost certainly ringworm. The diagnosis for some types of ringworm is simple, if spectacular: the dog is examined in a darkened room with an ultra-violet lamp, and if ringworm is present, the affected areas of skin will fluoresce – to see one's dog glowing in the dark is an unforgettable experience! However, note that some strains of ringworm do not fluoresce, and for these, diagnosis is based on growing and identifying the fungus in the laboratory.

The dog should be examined for skin changes once a week, and the obvious time to do this is when you groom him. Running your hands over his body will reveal any abnormalities that lie beneath; more detailed examination requires the hair to be systematically parted and the skin observed. Any raised area should be investigated, as should crusty or moist patches.

### Atopy

Atopic dogs become hypersensitive to substances such as grass, pollens or house-dust mites: these are called allergens. A test can be performed to identify the triggers in an individual dog, and then a special vaccine is made. This is called immunotherapy, and is effective in about 60 per cent of cases. Other treatments, such as antihistamines and essential fatty acids, can be effective, although sometimes a course of corticosteroids is necessary to give the dog relief. Sometimes a special diet will be prescribed to rule out food allergies as a cause of the

problem. In the first instance the dog will often chew its feet.

## Parasites

The days when dogs were flea-ridden and worm-infested are in the past, but even the most well kept, royally bred dogs are susceptible.

### Fleas

The dog will be scratching, and fleas are usually detected from their droppings in the coat when the dog is combed. Dogs become sensitive to flea saliva, and some develop a severe allergic reaction.

To control these pests, not only must the affected dog be treated, but also his blanket and the carpet on which he sleeps. His canine companions also need treatment. Flea dirt is composed of dried blood, and a good test of whether or not your dog has fleas is to deposit the contents of the comb on to wet paper: if fleas are present, their dirt will show as flecks of blood.

### Lice

When I first owned Goldens, over forty years ago, lice infestation was the greatest problem for breeders. I once saw a litter so badly affected that there was no single area on the puppies' heads that wasn't infested with lice – so great was the collection of these parasites that the puppy's ears stood out on both sides, pushed forwards by the mass of lice in their fur. The breeder had not noticed the problem!

Treat by washing with the appropriate preparation, or by spraying. It is important that the treatment is repeated after a fortnight to kill the hatching lice.

### Ticks

These are easily mistaken for warts, because initially they appear as small greyish-blue protruberances. Unlike warts, they grow very rapidly, as they feed on the dog's blood.

Examination with a hand lens will show the legs of the tick at the point where the mouthparts are embedded in the dog's skin.

The urge to pull the tick off the skin should be resisted, because the body will come away, leaving the mouthparts still embedded in the skin, and this will result in a sore, infected area. Ear drops containing an anti-parasitic component may be dabbed on to the tick, which will cause it to release its hold. Another effective method of removal is to cover the tick with olive oil: this will block the breathing spaces, so causing the tick to release its hold; after an hour the tick can be gently rotated, and it will come away intact.

Dogs exercised where sheep graze are at risk from ticks. Hedgehogs are more likely to be the cause in gardens, and my dogs certainly contract them in this way.

### Lyme Disease

Dogs may develop Lyme disease after being bitten by ticks carrying the Borrelia virus, though in the UK this is a rare occurrence; it does, however, happen more commonly in the USA. Unfortunately the symptoms exhibited by dogs affected with this disease do not instantly identify the problem: these include stiff joints, a raised temperature and loss of appetite.

When the disease is diagnosed early enough, antibiotics are used successfully. Dogs should be washed regularly with an anti-parasitic preparation if they are known to be at risk.

### Mange

Until recently, the regular use of washes virtually eradicated infestations by these parasitic mites. However, now that stringent control exists regarding the use of such chemicals, there has been a resurgence of the problem.

### Sarcoptic Mange

Also known as scabies, this condition causes the skin to become thickened and red. Black pigmented skin and hair loss results when animals are left untreated.

A blood test for antibodies to sarcoptes is about 95 per cent reliable if the dog has been infested for a week or two. There is a spot-on treatment for sarcoptes, and also an effective wash. Other dogs that have been in contact with those affected must be treated. The mites also cause irritation to humans.

### Cheyletiella

Also called 'walking dandruff', these mites live on the dog's hairs, visiting the skin to feed. When hairs from affected dogs are viewed through a magnifying lens, the tiny mites may be clearly seen moving about. These mites may be transmitted to other dogs and to humans.

### Demodex

Demodectic mange mites live mainly in the hair follicles. They may damage the skin, but appear to cause minimal irritation to the dog; however, they may cause severe hair loss. When present in the Golden Retriever this condition may suggest a problem with the immune system. Puppies are thought to acquire the infestation from their mothers.

## Worms

Since it has become the norm to dose the bitch for worms before mating and during pregnancy, the incidence of worm-ridden puppies has been reduced. Nevertheless, it should be remembered that although the serious and the more conscientious breeders employ this stringent method of control, there will be many other litters produced where breeders do not, and the worm burden of the puppies is severe.

### Roundworm

The life-cycle of the roundworm is complex. The eggs are passed in the faeces of infected animals, and require from three weeks to many months to be infective. The eggs are capable of remaining in vegetation or in the soil until they are ingested by licking. When the eggs are thus swallowed by the dog, they will hatch in the intestines, the larvae migrating first to the liver and then to the lungs. They pass through the trachea into the intestines, where they become egg-laying adults. This is the way eggs migrate in the young puppy. In puppies over three months of age the larvae will remain in the bloodstream instead of entering the lungs.

The body tissue of adult dogs will play host to dormant larvae, except pregnant bitches about to whelp, where the larvae will be migrating to the intestines via the lungs again.

Around the sixth week of pregnancy, some of the dormant larvae will infect the unborn puppies via the placenta. During the first weeks of suckling, the larvae will transfer to the puppies via their mother's milk.

Puppies with a heavy worm burden will not develop well, which is hardly surprising. Litters must be dosed regularly to prevent the recurrence of infestation, as worm eggs are amazingly resistant to cleaning and disinfection. This worming programme should be continued regularly up to a year old, and then twice a year. Breeders should be aware that some worming preparations (anthelmintics) will bring away whole worms and a bundle of what looks like spaghetti, while others will mascerate the worms so that nothing is visible. It is important not to assume that because there are no visible signs of worms, that the dog is not affected.

**Tapeworms**

Affected dogs often exhibit what appear to be flattened grains of rice stuck to the fur surrounding the anus; these are segments of tapeworms that have broken off. The tapeworm needs to be ingested by the flea or louse to develop, which makes it all the more important to keep the dog's coat free from external parasites.

Tapeworm infestation in dogs is less common than roundworm, and in forty years of keeping dogs the only tapeworms I have seen were in Egypt, where every stray dog was affected.

## The Nervous System

Epilepsy occurs when the nervous activity of the brain is disturbed, and such disturbances may last only seconds, or for as long as many minutes or even hours. The epileptic fit may be recognized as recurrent seizures, with no obvious trigger; having no known cause, they are described as 'idiopathic'. Epilepsy is believed to have an inherited component in some breeds, of which the Golden Retriever is one, although how it is inherited remains unknown. Such seizures are more common in males, and generally occur between six months and five years of age.

In the 1970s and 1980s many breeders were accused of hiding the fact that their dogs had epilepsy; however, it is possible that these breeders were not concealing the fact, but were simply unaware of it. During this period kennels were large and dogs were kept outside, and so went unobserved for many hours; as most attacks occur during the hours of darkness, the owners wouldn't have known about the seizures. Those with only one or two dogs kept indoors would probably notice the signs, whereas the owners of ten or more dogs would be less likely to observe the changes.

Although the mode of inheritance has not been proved, it is important that dogs and bitches suffering any type of seizure should not be bred from.

## Digestive Problems

### Diarrhoea

Diarrhoea affects all dogs and puppies at some time, and whereas a bout of diarrhoea in the adult will not be a serious problem, the opposite is true when it affects puppies.

It is diffcult to wean puppies without episodes of diarrhoea occurring; usually the cause is either the change of food or overeating. Diarrhoea that persists in puppies for more than a day needs veterinary intervention, because they will become rapidly dehydrated. As soon as diarrhoea is noticed, food should be withheld. A supply of clean water should always be available. The first meal given after a period of fasting is vitally important, and any temptation to offer the usual dog food should be avoided. I give boiled white fish and plain rice, as this is bland and unlikely to exacerbate the problem; it is suitable food for both puppies and adults.

Examine diarrhoea for traces of blood, and observe if it is bright red or black; this will assist your vet in making a diagnosis. Always take care when changing a dog's food, as sudden change will almost certainly trigger episodes of diarrhoea. Any change should be made over at least a week.

### Bloat

Bloat describes a distension of the abdomen, and is a condition common in deeper-chested breeds, such as setters, German Shepherds and Great Danes; however, the Golden Retriever is not exempt. Sometimes the signs are not easy to spot and may be nothing more than the dog looking restless; however, as the condition progresses, the dog will be in obvious pain.

The stomach, when full of gas, will twist where it connects to the oesophagus by 180 degrees. This frequently follows the drinking of large quantities of water after eating dry food. Feeding immediately before or after exercise is inadvisable, and is a suspected cause. The twist at the meeting of the oesophagus and stomach means that no gas can escape from the hugely distended stomach.

Treatment is sometimes effected with the use of a stomach tube, through which gas may escape, but this will not be successful if the stomach has twisted. Another possibility is to insert a wide bore needle through the ribs, into the abdomen, so allowing the gas to be released. Often the condition is resolved by surgery, to empty the stomach of gas and then staple it to the abdominal wall, to prevent future twisting.

This condition is extremely serious, and requires *immediate* veterinary treatment if the death of the dog is to be avoided. Frequently the signs are not noticed until sadly it is too late.

### Vomiting

Management of the dog that vomits is similar to that of the dog with diarrhoea: withhold food, and while water must be available, offer it in small quantities at regular intervals. After vomiting, dogs are prone to taking large drinks, which will immediately induce further episodes.

Notice the colour and content of the vomit as an aid to veterinary diagnosis. If it contains matter you cannot readily identify, collect a sample for analysis. Goldens are the world's greatest sock eaters, so check if any garments are missing; if they have ingested anything like this it must be removed as rapidly as possible, because such items may wrap around the gut, with dire consequences. They also love dishcloths and tea towels, so always ensure that these are out of reach.

## Urinary Problems

### Cystitis

Cystitis is a painful condition involving the urinary tract. The first signs of a dog being affected are repeated attempts to urinate, and only producing minute quantities each time; severely affected dogs will squat every few minutes. This is a serious condition needing rapid treatment with antibiotics; a urine sample should be taken with your dog to the vet. Usually an injection to calm the activity of the bladder will be given, alongside a long-lasting painkiller and antibiotics. Bitches appear to be more commonly affected than males, and recurring episodes are frequently seen.

## Eclampsia

Lactating bitches that suffer a drop in their blood calcium levels when their offspring are making great demands on their milk supply may exhibit this most alarming of conditions. Bitches that are affected appear generally unsettled and have a high temperature; they may twitch and have convulsions and collapse. The urgency of *immediate* veterinary treatment cannot be over-emphasized, because unless calcium is given intravenously, the bitch will die.

There are several contributing factors to this condition, but modern research suggests that supplementing the bitch's diet with calcium causes the natural extraction from the bones to be suppressed. The lignin present in high-fibre diets is also a contributing factor.

Once the owner has seen a bitch with eclampsia he will never forget it – but neither will he forget the immediate improvement that takes place once the calcium has been administered intravenously. It should be noted that calcium given by mouth will be totally ineffective.

If you suspect eclampsia, veterinary treatment is needed *immediately*. Any delay would almost certainly result in the death of the bitch.

### Pyometra

An infection of the uterus, pyometra may occur at any time, but is most commonly seen up to eight weeks after a bitch has been in season. The first signs are increased thirst and a raised temperature, and the dog is reluctant to eat, generally lethargic, and vomiting.

There are two forms of pyometra, known as 'open' or 'closed'. In the former, a discharge appears from the vulva; with the latter, the discharge will not be seen for several days, being retained within the closed cervix.

Treatment is sometimes attempted with antibiotics, but in most cases the bitch will need a hysterectomy as soon as possible. When antibiotics are used, before resorting to surgery, they appear to be effective, but once they are withdrawn, the condition usually returns. Bitches recover from surgery remarkably well, provided there is no delay once the symptoms have been diagnosed.

## General Observations

A good dog owner is an observant one. A vet once remarked to me that if a dog looked all right, then he probably was all right. While there is some truth in that statement, health is not only about appearance: it is frequently a deviation from normal behaviour that will alert the owner to the fact that something is wrong. The dog that runs to the door every morning, desperate to go out, obviously has a problem if he fails to do this one morning.

I work by the following rules: provided that my dogs are not vomiting or having diarrhoea, are eating well, show no signs of lameness, want to go for their walks, have no unpleasant odour and no discharge from any orifice, then they can have little wrong. It must be remembered that dogs, compared to humans, are stoic, and it is this very stoicism that may sometimes mask an underlying, serious condition.

We each know our own dogs, and what is normal for some, would be positively abnormal for others. Be observant, as the secret of good animal husbandry is to spot symptoms at the onset of their development. Most conditions are far easier to treat successfully if detected early.

## Insurance

For the owner who has one or two dogs, insurance is probably a good idea, but for the person who owns several, the cost becomes prohibitive. If you choose to insure some and not all your dogs, you can be sure that the one that becomes ill and incurs the highest veterinary bill is the one that isn't insured. Deciding whether or not to insure a dog is tantamount to juggling: insurance premiums are expensive, but so is veterinary treatment. It is impossible to advise whether or not owners should insure their dogs, as financial circumstances differ.

If you decide to insure your dog, shop around before deciding which policy best suits your needs. Ideally talk to those who have dogs covered by the one you are thinking of using, and note their opinions. Check what one company offers as compared with the rest, because they differ widely; for example, some will not insure dogs over a certain age, while others will, but the premium increases markedly as the dog ages. Working on the premise that the older the dog, the more likely he is to need treatment, it may be worth paying a little extra to cover old age.

Some companies will pay for prescription diets, which is an excellent arrangement if your dog has a condition requiring this in the long term. One of my dogs has an absorption problem for which a prescription diet is required. Given that it costs just under £50 each month, and my dog could live for fourteen years, this presents a considerable financial commitment.

If you are thinking of breeding, check that your policy covers this. Also check that it covers inherited conditions, as many do not.

Some will only pay for a single treatment of a condition, whilst others will provide cover for return visits to the vet for the same condition. Consider the cost if a dog were found to be diabetic and needed insulin for the rest of its life. Covering such a dog by insurance would be a sound option – although be aware that you cannot insure dogs for an existing condition.

Insurance companies differ in their definition of 'accident', so if you live alongside a main road, ensure that injuries resulting from road traffic accidents are covered. I know of at least one company that will not pay for treatment following such accidents, maintaining they are the result of the owner's negligence.

If you own several dogs, consider the 'breeders' or 'block' policies, which could be cheaper than insuring animals individually.

Owners should also consider insurance that provides cover in the event of their dogs biting or causing an accident. We live in a highly litigious society, where taking someone to court is the automatic reaction following an accident – and such cases are incredibly costly. A few dog clubs offer insurance at reduced rates to their members, and such cover is usually well worth considering.

Before embarking on such insurance, check whether your household policy covers you for such eventualities.

# 9 The Old Dog

*A thirteen-year-old bitch showing the greying face of old age.*

The Golden Retriever is relatively long lived, and it is not unusual for it to reach fifteen. Most remain healthy and active until they pass their tenth year, after which signs associated with advancing age become evident. Older dogs sleep for longer periods, only waking when it is time for food or for the next outing; they also become less supple when rising after a period of prolonged rest. The stiffness often becomes obvious in the hind legs, and the dog will shuffle and make several attempts to stand, rather than rising in one fluid movement. Later there appears to be less stability in the forelegs, and the same laboured action is seen on rising.

## Exercise for the Elderly Dog

To stop exercising dogs that exhibit stiffness would exacerbate the problem. It is the type of exercise which is important, and generally old dogs will leave their owners in no doubt as to when they have had enough. Years ago, one of my old dogs decided he'd had enough when I attempted the walk home from a visit to the vet's surgery. No amount of pleading would persuade him to get to his feet, and eventually I rang my husband to bring the car. The ostensibly exhausted Sparky summoned suffcient energy to leap in unaided!

Gentle walks are preferred to cross-country hikes, and an old dog that persists in dashing around is probably better kept on a lead for part of the walk. Avoid throwing things for an elderly dog to retrieve, because running after a ball will cause too much stress on old joints, and never throw sticks, as many fatalities occur each year when the dog lands on the stick, which then pierces the mouth or throat.

*These two thirteen-year-olds still enjoy walks.*

Walking on grass is easier on the joints of both dogs and humans than walking on a hard surface. It is also more enjoyable for dogs, as grass carries many scents.

Being stiff need not mean the end of walks for your dog, nor should it mean that he experiences pain for the rest of his life. There are many remedies available now, which, given regularly, have amazingly successful results. There are liquids, tablets and injections, and there is definitely one to suit each dog. Dogs with ultra-sensitive digestion cannot tolerate some of these medicines, but it is important to persevere, as there will be one type that suits your dog. I have an old dog that cannot tolerate one brand given as tablets, but it suits her perfectly when given by injection.

Sometimes a large dose is needed for several days initially in order to make stiff, inflamed joints pain free and supple, but this can usually be reduced to a maintenance dose, which is given for the rest of the dog's life.

## Travelling the Older Dog

Older dogs will need help getting in and out of cars. Over twenty years ago I bought a folding ramp, and it has been the most useful piece of equipment I have ever owned. These ramps are very stable when placed on the sill of the car's tailgate. It helps to train dogs to use a ramp while they are still young, so that when they eventually need to use it they are fully accustomed to doing so. Train dogs to walk on it while it is flat on the ground, then raise it slightly, and they will still walk with confidence. They are more wary about coming down than going up, and a little persuasion is generally needed – a biscuit held in front of the dog, in the manner of donkey and carrot, invariably works. The surface of wooden ramps can be improved by tacking on a piece of carpet; the metal variety usually

*A ramp is invaluable for helping an old dog get in and out of the car.*

has a piece of fleecy bedding screwed on, which may be removed for washing.

## Diet for the Ageing Dog

Other signs of ageing are that the digestive system is less able to deal adequately with some foods. You will find that the complete diet that suited your dog for the last ten years now gives him bouts of diarrhoea. Go for a rice-based food and a lower protein content, as a body that is not producing the action

*Raising the dish makes eating easier for old dogs.*

needs less fuel. Another of my old dogs has suddenly developed an intolerance to wheat gluten; sometimes simply using a gluten-free food will cure all sorts of digestive problems.

The Golden does not, in general, tolerate milk well, and even those who have found it acceptable in their youth and during the middle years, frequently exhibit an intolerance as they age. Whole milk is poorly tolerated at all stages.

Sometimes it is the volume of food that old dogs find diffcult to deal with, so instead of giving one meal a day, divide the quantity into three more easily digested portions.

Raising the feeding and drinking bowls helps dogs that find it diffcult to lower their heads, and this also has the advantage of reducing the air intake as they eat. Raised stands are readily and cheaply available, but a substitute may be made by placing the dish on a rubber mat on a stool.

The coats of old dogs also change: usually they become dry, but very occasionally they can become greasy. A dry coat can be helped by adding olive oil to the food, and giving primrose oil capsules; there are also conditioners that can be combed into the fur. The greasy coat is cured by bathing with shampoos formulated to control the problem.

## Grooming

Be gentle when grooming old dogs. My youngsters enjoy a vigorous brushing, but the oldies visibly wince. Avoid the steel-pinned slicker brushes on an old, sensitive skin – try them on your own hair and you'll see how abrasive they are. If you can hear your brush strokes, then you are brushing too hard. Use steel combs gently as they are very scratchy.

## Bedding

There is a wonderful array of bedding available for pets, ranging from elaborate canine settees to heated pads and duvets. My preference is for the thick quilts that are fully washable, complete with easily removed covers. Bedding will smell unless you wash it regularly. My dogs are bathed regularly for shows

*The coat of old dogs alters in texture.*

*Old dogs appreciate a thick bed away from draughts.*

so have no body odour, but their bedding smells 'doggy' unless I change it every three days, or even more frequently in muddy weather.

Ensure that the size you choose fits into your washer easily. A friend treated her dogs to super-sized duvets, only to find she had to take them to the laundrette in town because they would only fit into a commercial washer! Choose fabric that is warm to the touch and dries easily; your elderly dog might look cute on pink satin, but it is slippery, cold to the touch, and does not repel stains.

If your dog normally sleeps in the middle of a room, move his bed into a corner, preferably near a radiator. A guard might be necessary to stop him lying right up against a very hot radiator.

## Maintaining Good Health

### Eyes

The eyes of an older dog sometimes take on a cloudy appearance; this is quite different from hereditary cataract described elsewhere. Eyes will water more, and a moistened tissue will remove deposits that would otherwise collect in eye corners.

### Nails

The nails of old dogs grow at an alarming rate. Even those that have remained naturally short throughout the dog's life suddenly take on this increased growth, and frequently

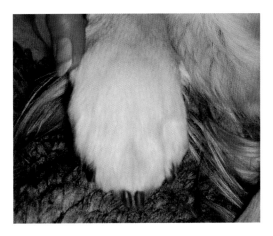

*The nails of old dogs grow very quickly.*

137

*Dew claws will grow full circle unless regularly trimmed.*

become coarser and more brittle in texture. These factors make them more prone to breaking and splitting, and a broken nail may come away and reveal the soft 'quick' inside; however, this will shrink back naturally without veterinary intervention.

It is a fallacy to believe that dogs exercised on hard surfaces keep their nails short. Mine are exercised on grass, and some have the shortest nails while others have growth resembling talons!

The dew claws of old dogs grow faster than the other nails, and if left will grow in a circle and into the flesh. When trimming these, and all nails, ensure that only the dead ends are removed and that you do not cut the 'quick', as this will bleed profusely and cause the dog pain.

### Ears

The ears of an old dog produce more wax than during the dog's younger years. Canine wax is dark brown, almost black, and any excess should be removed with the moist tissues used for babies. Never poke cotton buds into the ear, because dogs tend to move unexpectedly, and a jerk of the head just as you have inserted a cotton bud could perforate the ear drum. I cut away excess fur from where the ear flap joins the head and neck, as this allows air to circulate more freely and reduces the build-up of heat inside the ear. If you keep more than one dog, they are frequently adept at cleaning each other's ears!

## Behaviour Change

As dogs age they sometimes exhibit bizarre behaviour, reminiscent of Alzheimer's disease in humans. Old dogs will bark in the night for no apparent reason, and when the light is turned on they will be seen standing in the middle of the room, looking bewildered. Others will suddenly decide it is feeding time when they have only recently been fed, and will lie in front of their dishes, barking like mad. Some appear to see things and stare into space, as if in a trance.

Nothing can be done to alleviate this strange behaviour (which generally worsens with advancing years); all you can do is offer reassurance by stroking and talking to the dog until the 'episode' has passed.

## The Final Service

However well you attend to your elderly companion's needs it is not possible to halt the symptoms of advancing years. There will come a time when you have done everything possible to improve your dog's life and comfort, but it becomes obvious that his quality of life is impaired. This is the time you are able to provide the final act of kindness for your much loved friend.

To have a dog put to sleep is never easy (I write with the act fresh in my mind, having just said goodbye to a fifteen-year-old), but it is what we, as dog lovers, must do. I always request my vet to come to the house, so there is as little stress as possible for the dog, and the journey to the surgery is avoided. The process involves a single injection, administered into a vein in the dog's leg; it is very quick, and by the time the plunger of the syringe is fully depressed, the dog has slipped quietly away. Do not be tempted to ask for your dog to be given a sedative first, mistakenly thinking this will make the process easier, as it will delay the action of the lethal injection, so prolonging the whole event.

### Burial or Cremation?

Decide in advance what you wish to do with your dog's body after death. All mine rest here in the orchard, and I frequently have a quiet word with them when I'm gardening. For practical reasons, a garden burial might not be possible, so cremation is an alternative. I personally find it distasteful, but had to employ this method for a much loved dog when local flooding made burial impossible.

Cremation is arranged either through your vet, or independently with one of the many companies who now offer this. It is expensive, but a very professional service is offered. They will collect the dog and after a week the ashes will be returned to you. You will be

*Your pet's remains will be returned to you in the container of your choice.*

offered a choice of containers for your pet's remains, ranging from a simple wooden box to an elaborate urn, bearing your dog's name and their date of birth and death.

*A chapel of rest is provided by most pet crematoria.*

---

### Dealing with Grief

Grief after losing a much loved dog is as real as that experienced after the death of a human. We all deal with grief differently, but there are various self-help exercises, and these can lessen the feeling of unbearable loss. Collecting together the photographs of your dog, and placing them in an album or arranging them in one of the many albums offered on the various computer photographic programs, is helpful: by so doing you are focusing on the happy occasions you both enjoyed.

Children who mourn the loss of a pet can be encouraged to compile a journal of stories, drawings and photographs. Again, it is the joy of owning the dog which is highlighted, rather than the anguish of loss. Watching videos of your dog also helps, as does simply talking about him, preferably with someone who knew him really well.

Counselling following pet bereavement is offered throughout Britain. It is important to find someone skilled, and vets will advise and recommend such a person. I used professional help many years ago when a young bitch I adored was killed by other dogs. So great was my grief that I couldn't work, and just ceased to function. When you simply cannot deal with the sadness of loss on your own, it makes good sense to involve professionals who can help.

I have friends who proudly display these containers, and one has left instructions that they should eventually be interred with her. When my dog was cremated I eventually buried her ashes in the orchard, alongside the other dogs.

During the last decade, pet cemeteries have appeared throughout Britain. These are tastefully organized, with graves in rows, like human burial grounds. Some charge a standard fee for collection and burial, whereas others charge for annual maintenance. These cemeteries can provide the solution for those without gardens and who wish to have their pets buried.

## And Finally...

To conclude on a happier note, we must accept that death is a part of life, and certainly a part of owning dogs. Dogs live for a very short while compared with us, so it is obvious that we will suffer their loss many times during our association with them. But had we not had them in the first place, we should have been denied the intense pleasure and joy of owning them; so on balance, any distress experienced must be considered worthwhile.

*Dogs live for a very short time compared with us, and become more special as they age.*

# Acknowledgements

My thanks to the following for allowing their photographs to be used: Heather and Mike Berry; Sue and Kevin Binks; Fiona Brighley; Dawn Childs; Rosemary Cowper MRCVS; Jim Crosbie; David Dalton; Stuart Ellis BVSc.CertV.Opthal.MRCVS; Elysian Fields Pet Crematorium; Olga Fitton; Andrew Hird; the Kennel Club Picture Library; Graham Morgan; Dr Larry Roberts MRCVS; Jackie and Mick Rogerson; Bernard Slattery; Michael Trafford; Celia Tricoglus; Stewart Weller; Lesley Wilson; Tina and Ian Witty; and Catherine and Sven Zingg.

Thanks also to Rosemary Cowper for proof-reading and advising on Chapter 8; Maureen Hartley for typing the manuscript; and J. and D. Stirling and Jessie Harrow for historical background.

# Index